DEFYING THE HOLOCAUST

Ten courageous Christians who supported Jews

Tim Dowley

First published in Great Britain in 2020

Society for Promoting Christian Knowledge
36 Causton Street
London SW1P 4ST
www.spck.org.uk

British Library Cataloguing-in-Publication Data
A catalogue record for this book is available from the British Library

ISBN 978–0–281–08362–6
eBook ISBN 978–0–281–08363–3

1 3 5 7 9 10 8 6 4 2

Typeset by Manila Typesetting Company
Printed in Great Britain by Jellyfish Print Solutions

eBook by Manila Typesetting Company

Produced on paper from sustainable forests

For Mariette Demuth née Bonda (b. 23 May 1934, Prague)
and Walter Demuth (b. 18 January 1932, Frankfurt-am-Main)

Out of the depths I cry to you, O Lord.
Lord, hear my voice!

Psalm 130.1, *De Profundis*

Contents

Preface   ix
Prologue   xi

Introduction   1
The Nazi Holocaust: a short timeline   11
 1 A most unorthodox nun   22
 2 Pestilent priests   49
 3 The borders of heaven   74
 4 No hiding place   104
 5 Quakers and U-boats   124
 6 The constant midwife   148
 7 The monk on a bicycle   164
 8 The Vatican Pimpernel   180
 9 Committed Swedes   201
10 An elusive missionary   219

Bibliography   235
Index   239

Preface

It is of course difficult to write about the Holocaust because of its dark nature; but it is vitally important. Not for nothing does Laurence Rees subtitle his book *The Nazis* 'A warning from history'.[1]

For stories such as those retold here, it can sometimes be difficult to be precise about times, dates, numbers and even names. For rescuers and escapers to have kept contemporaneous records of their activities would of course have been extremely hazardous, if not foolhardy: such documents would have been gold dust to the SS, the Gestapo and other oppressors. In any event, the helpers themselves were often so absorbed and exhausted by their work to the exclusion of any other activities that keeping log-books or writing journals would not only have been dangerous but could also have stolen valuable time and energy from their vital core activities.

In the absence of extensive records by rescuers, many of these stories depend largely on memories and accounts recorded or archived later, whether immediately after the war or during the decades that followed. Sometimes memories have faded or details have merged. I have depended largely upon secondary sources in the form of published books, articles and digital records, comparing and analysing, and attempting to apply balanced, careful judgement in recounting these extraordinary stories. I have tried as far as possible to select

---

1 BBC Books, London, 1997.

what appear to be the most reliable sources, and have looked for confirmation by two or more witnesses where available.

Accounts in books published after the war can sometimes seem unintentionally to inflate the numbers of those rescued or exaggerate the results of an individual rescuer or group. I have been anxious here to avoid romanticizing or embellishing stories that by their nature are already singular in the heights and depths of the human experience and behaviour they describe, determined that this be history rather than hagiography.

Despite my best efforts, there probably remain unintended errors of inclusion and exclusion, of numbers and dates: I can only apologize in advance and ask the reader's indulgence. Should there be a second edition, I hope corrections can be made.

I have received generous help from a number of people in writing this book. My thanks go in particular to: Ben Barkow and the staff of the Wiener Library; Martina Voigt and staff at the Silent Heroes Memorial Center (*Gedenkstätte Stille Helden*), Berlin; the British Library and its virtually inexhaustible resources; Dr Rosamunde Codling, Archivist at Surrey Chapel, Norwich; Jerry O'Grady, Chair of the O'Flaherty Memorial Society; Willie Watkins for his patient guiding in Berlin; Christopher Braun for his helpful insights into Quakerism; the Norwich Record Office; Matthew Aitken, Colin Mitchell and the Dunscore Heritage Centre; and Daniel Guy for his careful reading and commentary . . . And of course to my family: of all the books I have written, I have been immersed most deeply in this. My love and gratitude go to all of them as I emerge from that process.

Tim Dowley
Dulwich, London

Prologue

He who saves one life, it is as if he saved an entire world.
(Talmud Sanhedrin 37a)

In October 1938, Nazi Germany forced Czechoslovakia to surrender its German-speaking region known as Sudetenland, an action infamously dismissed by the British Prime Minister Neville Chamberlain as 'a quarrel in a far-away country between people of whom we know nothing'. It was almost immediately clear that Hitler's appetite would not be satiated by this victory: in March 1939 he completed what he called the peaceful 'liquidation' of Czechoslovakia.

On 16 March 1939, the day after the Germans occupied Prague, a Jewish man named Leo Bonda departed from Czechoslovakia for Paris, leaving behind his wife, Liesl, and two young children, seven-year-old Jean and four-year-old Mariette. Liesl was arrested soon afterwards and held in prison for five weeks, until her uncle managed successfully to negotiate her release by the German authorities. One freezing January night in 1940 Liesl and her two children left Prague by train, seen off by relatives who included the children's uncle, the expressionist playwright Paul Kornfeld (1889–1942), who was later to die in the Holocaust.

The three travelled first to Genoa, in northern Italy, where they spent three months attempting to obtain visas. In April 1940 they journeyed on to Paris, where they were reunited with Leo. Just two months later, on 14 June 1940, the Germans occupied the City of Light and the family had to move on again. Leo bought a lorry and they drove south to the unoccupied Vichy sector of France, travelling by night and sleeping by day. Finally they arrived at St-Romain-et-St-Clément in the Dordogne, a tiny hamlet of around 20 houses where the mayor was encouraging his neighbours to harbour Jewish refugees. Leo managed to rent a flat comprising a living room, bedroom and small kitchen. All the villagers were aware that a Jewish family had arrived in their midst and eventually someone denounced them. The family now had to move on in a hurry yet again, to the village of Sarran in the Corrèze, where Leo was forced to work on the land.

At dawn on 26 August 1942 there was a major round-up of Jews, a *rafle*: Jean and Mariette escaped by hiding in a field of Jerusalem artichokes, their parents by concealing themselves in a haystack. For ten days the family managed to survive in a nearby forest, after which the children were given refuge at the Château de Chabannes, a home for Jewish children run by the OSE,[2] a Jewish organization that rescued children from the Nazis. Their staple diet was lentils, though the children even ate raw potatoes that they picked up in the fields. Meanwhile Liesl and Leo moved from farm to farm, staying wherever they could find people willing to help them.

With the help of the Resistance, and using forged ID, on 12 October the Bondas drove 40 kilometres to Grenoble, near the Swiss border, hidden under furniture on the back of a lorry. A helper took them to a hotel where he knew they wouldn't be

---

2 *Oeuvre de secours aux enfants* ('Relief Work for Children').

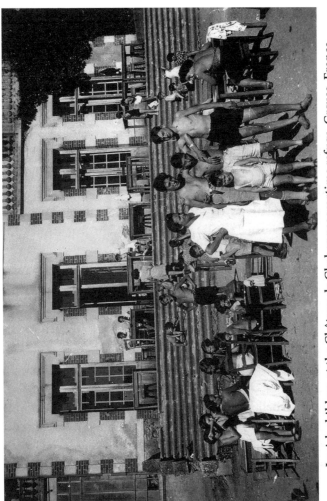

Jewish children at the Château de Chabannes wartime refuge, Creuse, France

required to register their names. In constant fear of a raid by the Nazis or by the collaborating French police, they slept in a different bed most nights, until eventually a woman offered to rent them a room for three months. Friends in the Resistance provided forged identity cards and ration cards and warned them if a police raid was imminent, though Leo and Liesl rarely ventured out.

Everything went relatively safely until March 1943, when Leon heard that Jean and Mariette were in danger because children and teachers at Chabannes were being deported to the East. A helper went to fetch the children and found the family a flat in a poorer section of Grenoble, where they were able to live relatively unnoticed under the assumed name of 'Bour'. They buried the ID papers with their true names, for retrieval after Liberation.

On 15 August 1944 they heard an announcement on the radio that the Allies had arrived in Provence. A local pastor came to tell them that the Germans would now stop fighting. On the morning of 22 August, with the city covered in tricolours, the Bondas watched the victorious Allies march in. Soldiers threw chocolates, sweets, cigarettes and chewing gum to the watching children. Little Mariette kissed at least 20 GIs.

Mariette believes the man who helped them in Grenoble was André Girard-Clot (1897–1944), whose family owned a textile and lingerie shop. He belonged to the Reformed Church of Grenoble, where he worked closely as a layman (a *conseil presbytéral*) with pastors Charles Westphal (1896–1972) and Jean Cook (1899–1973). Cook and Westphal hid fugitives in their church and encouraged local families to take in Jewish refugees. Westphal outspokenly condemned the anti-Semitism of the Vichy government, helped Jews escape to Switzerland, and intervened with the prefecture, the police and later the Gestapo in an effort to protect Jews and other fugitives. He also helped reform French Protestant attitudes towards the Jews and after the war was named, jointly with his wife, Denise, as among Yad Vashem's 'Righteous Among the Nations'.

André Girard-Clot had been badly injured in the First World War and – like his wife – belonged to an old Protestant family. This couple are said to have helped save 32 Jewish families, concealing them in their shop or home for anything from a day to several weeks. The Girard-Clots sometimes hid people in their warehouse on the shop's first floor or behind textiles in the showroom. The shop stood on a corner of the boulevard Edouard-Rey in the centre of Grenoble, and had entrances on two different streets, enabling fugitives to enter by one door and escape unobserved by the other.

André also supported a *maquis* resistance group of six theology students from Montpellier who set up camp in nearby hills in the summer of 1943. Each weekend he set out with a backpack filled with food and clothing for the camp, returning with letters for the students' friends and relatives. Eventually an informer led German soldiers to the camp; Girard-Clot was arrested when they discovered his address. Imprisoned by the Gestapo at Montluc Prison, Lyon, he was condemned to death by the infamous Klaus Barbie. Girard-Clot's sentence was subsequently commuted, and he was deported first to Compiègne and then to Mauthausen concentration camp, Austria, where he died in the infirmary on 2 May 1944.

Introduction

In the end, it is all about memory, its sources and its
magnitude, and, of course, its consequences.
(Elie Wiesel, *Night*, 1960)

At least 11 million died in the concentration and death camp
system, and at least four million at Auschwitz/Birkenau alone.
The Nazis murdered approximately six million Jews and at least
another five million non-Jews. More than one million children
were murdered, many newborn or unborn. The system comprised major camps and hundreds of subsidiary camps,
stretching like giant malign spiderwebs across Europe.

It is vital that these figures are recorded and substantiated.
But so great are the numbers that it can be difficult to com-
prehend their devastating significance. In this book, I have
taken a step back and, rather than attempt another survey
of the entirety of the Holocaust,[1] I have selected the stories
of ten or so Christians from various church traditions and
denominations, and from a number of different countries,
operating in a multiplicity of situations with diverse outcomes.
I have not included accounts of larger groupings of rescuers
and helpers, such as the extraordinary efforts of the village

---

1   Authoritative recent accounts include: Laurence Rees, *The Holocaust*, Penguin,
    London, 2017; David Cesarani, *Final Solution: The fate of the Jews 1933–49*, Pan,
    London, 2017; Nikolaus Wachsmann, *KL: A history of the Nazi concentration
    camps*, Little, Brown, London, 2015.

of Le Chambon-sur-Lignon, France, or the priests of Assisi, Italy. This is partly because their histories have been amply and authoritatively told elsewhere, and also because the extent and complexity of these stories would be difficult to summarize adequately in a single chapter in a relatively short book.[2]

The English poet William Blake insisted, '[S]he who would do good to another must do it in Minute Particulars. General Good is the plea of the scoundrel, hypocrite and flatterer.'[3] The stories I have selected represent a mere handful from the accounts of thousands of individuals, groups and organizations who attempted to protect and rescue Jews and others from the Holocaust, but I hope to illustrate the diversity, ingenuity, courage and determination of some of the thousands of men and women involved.

Twelve trucks

To summarize the many targets of Hitler's Holocaust, one writer has helpfully used the image of a train consisting of 12 wagons, each wagon representing a different group selected for oppression and extermination. While this picture gives no concept of the incomprehensibly large numbers involved, or the relative size of the various groups, it does offer a graphic representation of the varieties of humanity assailed:

---

2   On Le Chambon-sur-Lignon see for instance Philip Hallie, *Lest Innocent Blood Be Shed: The story of the village of Le Chambon and how goodness happened there*, Harper & Row, New York, 1994; Patrick Henry, *We Only Know Men*, Catholic University of America Press, Washington D.C., 2007; Caroline Moorehead, *Village of Secrets*, Chatto & Windus, London, 2014; Peter Grose, *A Good Place to Hide*, Nicholas Brealey, London, 2016. For Assisi: Alexander Ramati, *The Assisi Underground: The priests who rescued Jews*, Stein and Day, New York, 1978.

3   *Jerusalem*, f. 55, ll. 48–53, 60–6, in *The Poetical Works*, 1908.

- From the first cattle truck emerge the Jews, wearing the yellow Star of David. Most are selected for instant extermination, others for forced hard labour or medical experimentation. The Holocaust was intended totally to eliminate all Jews.
- From the second truck come Romani and Sinti wearing a brown triangle, selected for their supposedly 'non-Aryan' characteristics. They are sent to a family camp to wait till the gas chambers are ready to eradicate them.
- From the third truck come male homosexuals. They are sent to Sachsenhausen concentration camp, near Oranienburg, north of Berlin, or to Buchenwald, near Weimar. The pink triangle they wear shows they have broken Germany's Paragraph 175, by committing sexual acts, kissing or simply embracing. Some will be offered an opportunity to 'reform' by sexual activity with a woman in the camp brothel. Most will be assaulted, raped and worked and beaten to death.
- From truck four emerge clergy, priests, nuns and lay people from many different Christian church traditions who have defied the Nazi creed and are 'guilty' of faith and decency. They wear a purple triangle. Some will be relatively favoured, some killed outright and others worked to death. The group includes Jehovah's Witnesses, who prioritized the Bible over the ideology of the Third Reich.[4] Between

---

4 Jehovah's Witnesses feel spiritual kinship towards the Jews as the people of the Old Testament and believe Christ died for humankind's sins – but not that Jewish guilt is linked to the crucifixion. In 1940 their paper *Das Goldene Zeitalter* declared: 'The present generation of Jews is in no way responsible for what the Pharisees and others did 1900 years ago.' The Witnesses saw Hitler as a demonic leader whose doctrines had to be challenged in defence of basic Christianity.

1933 and 1945 5,911 of the 6,034 Jehovah's Witnesses in
Nazi Germany were rounded up and sent to concentration
camps. Some were eventually released.

- From truck five come Russian prisoners of war, who are
  completely brutalized.
- From truck six emerge peoples the Nazis describe
  as 'sub-human': Poles, Slavs, Slovaks, Ukrainians,
  Lithuanians and Russians. They are forced to work on
  minimal rations and as a result most die.
- The seventh truck contains political prisoners, mostly
  Communists and Socialists, together with resistance fighters captured from across Europe. They are made to wear a
  red triangle.
- From the eighth truck come the disabled, who will be
  killed, their bodies stripped and skeletons analysed, their
  skulls studied by Nazi 'scientists'. Twins will be observed,
  tested and operated on by Dr Mengele and his like.
- The ninth truck unloads older women and men, the sick,
  the mentally ill and physically disabled with crutches and
  wheelchairs. All are sent straight to the gas chamber.
- From the tenth truck appear the deaf, dumb and blind.
- Out of truck eleven come criminals and some unfortunate
  people whom a particular Nazi just didn't like. They wear
  a green triangle.
- In the twelfth and final truck are pregnant women and
  children. Generally, as soon as a baby was delivered, both
  mother and child were sent to the gas chamber.

All these people faced brutal treatment, starvation, torture,
overwork and disease. The Nazis attacked the old, the sick, the

mentally ill, the deaf, the dumb, the blind and the crippled, and aimed to kill all Jews and most Gypsies. They classified as 'sub-human', persecuted and murdered Poles, Russians, Slavs and Soviet prisoners of war. They attacked those they regarded as 'odd', including the physically atypical, twins, hunchbacks and people with unusual skulls and skeletons. They targeted political opponents and attacked prisoners of conscience and dissident Christians, Jehovah's Witnesses, Eastern Orthodox Christians, Lutherans, Catholics, priests and pastors, male homosexuals, resistance fighters, women and children.[5]

The Nazis developed a toxic racial ideology that combined traditional Christian-based anti-Jewish prejudice and hatred with racial anti-Semitism and pseudo-scientific eugenics. Beyond this, Hitler believed the two most racially pure peoples were the Aryans and the Jews, between whom there was an existential struggle for existence. By the same racial theories, the Slavs were dismissed as inferior, 'born slaves'.

Heinrich Himmler had become head of the *Schutzstaffel*, or SS, in the early 1930s, when it was a squad of bodyguards, and proceeded to mould it into an elite group of Nazi believers. When the Second World War started, Himmler used the SS as his weapon in this 'racial struggle of pitiless severity', embarking on mass killings in Poland and the Soviet Union. At the famous 1942 Wannsee Conference, the SS emerged with the leading role in the execution of the 'Final Solution' through death camps and extermination squads.

---

5   From Kennilyn Fuig, 'Non-Jewish Victims in the Concentration Camps' in Michael Berenbaum, ed., *A Mosaic of Victims: Non-Jews persecuted and murdered by the Nazis*, New York University Press, New York, 1990, p. 176.

The helpers

When the Nazis started to destroy the European Jews, the millions of non-Jews in Europe had to decide their stance: would they help the Nazis, help the Jews, or do nothing? A very small percentage resisted or helped. The great majority did nothing. More than 16,000 rescuers have been recognized officially by Yad Vashem in Jerusalem, yet no one knows how many there were in total.

The number of those who escaped the Holocaust by living illegally with the aid and support of non-Jews is extremely low in comparison with the number deported to the extermination camps. For example, in Berlin some Gentiles were ready and able to risk rescuing Jews,[6] although they were very few compared with those who remained indifferent, looked the other way, became accomplices by denouncing people to the police or actively participated in the Holocaust.

It has often been wrongly assumed that all rescuers were Christian. In fact some were atheists or agnostics, some in south-eastern Europe were Muslims, and dedicated Communists also rescued Jews. Some rescuers had a Jewish friend, co-worker or colleague whom they wanted to help. Some were motivated by patriotism or politics: for example, the Danes aided the Jews of their country partly as an act of national resistance to the Nazis. Many of the rescuers acted out of a sense of justice or in straightforward response to the suffering of fellow humans.

Of the tiny minority who rescued Jews for explicitly Christian reasons, some did so from a particular sense of religious

---

6   See Chapters 5 and 9.

kinship, a sort of Christian philo-Semitism, apparently more often found among those within Calvinist traditions. Some Christians rescued Jews in response to the Bible's teaching on compassion, love and justice – for instance the story of the Good Samaritan, or the commandment to love God and one's neighbour – applying these precepts to the dreadful contemporary events. Some Christian leaders denounced the evils of Nazism and its murderous policies, teaching that it was a heresy, and inspiring Christians to participate in rescue activities. Most explicitly Christian rescuers were markedly devout.

It is risky to generalize from the small number of men and women whose stories have been selected for this book. However, it seems noteworthy that many were unmarried (several because they had taken a vow of celibacy); that a number were women; and that, apart from their astonishing acts of individual courage and initiative, most would probably not have found a place in history. The Polish philosopher Zygmunt Bauman (1925–2017) underlined this insight: 'were it not for the Holocaust, most of these helpers might have continued on their independent paths, some pursuing charitable actions, some leading simple, unobtrusive lives. They were dormant heroes, often indistinguishable from those around them.'[7] Nechama Tec (1931–), herself a Holocaust survivor, has suggested that many of the helpers were not motivated so much by altruism as by an unusual degree of independence: 'individuality and separateness from their environment'. Almost

---

7 Zygmunt Bauman, *Modernity and the Holocaust*, Polity Press, Cambridge, 1991, pp. 5–7.

all seem to have combined a steely strength of character with a certain contrariness and a warm humanity.

All the people whose stories are told in this book showed strong moral principles and lived by what they regarded as traditional Christian standards, probably with greater conscientiousness than many. Yet counterintuitively, when faced with the stark realities of Nazi cruelty and power, they surprised even themselves by contravening what previously they would have regarded as laws set in stone. For instance a Dutch rescuer named Marion Pritchard, née van Binsbergen, reckoned that, by the end of the war, she had 'killed, stolen, lied, everything. I had broken every one of the Ten Commandments, except maybe the first'.[8] Corrie ten Boom, whose story is told in Chapter 4, said much the same thing. As for why she helped, Pritchard claimed, 'I didn't think about it. I just did it.' Similarly Father Bruno, whose story is told in Chapter 7, said, 'I just did what I'm supposed to do.'

The Dutch Christian Joop Westerweel, who with his 'Westerweel group' succeeded in smuggling between 200 and 300 Jews across Belgium and France to neutral Switzerland and Spain, and who was executed by the Nazis on 11 August 1944, argued for action rather than debate, quoting Matthew 10.37–39:

Whoever loves father or mother more than me is not worthy of me; and whoever loves son or daughter more than me is not worthy of me; and whoever does not take

---

8 Malka Drucker and Gay Block, 'Marion P. van Binsbergen Pritchard', in *Rescuers: Portraits of moral courage in the Holocaust*, Holmes & Meier, New York, 1992, p. 36.

up the cross and follow me is not worthy of me. Those who find their life will lose it, and those who lose their life for my sake will find it.

(NRSV)

He and his wife, Wilhelmina, left their four children in the care of foster parents while they engaged in rescue work.

In reading these stories, it is important to keep the numbers of Christian rescuers in perspective. 'Some Christians did choose to stand with suffering Jews in the Holocaust. Many more Christians, however, chose to stare silently away from the flames while embracing twenty centuries of anti-Jewish theology.'[9]

Who are 'The Righteous'?

Located in Jerusalem, Yad Vashem (Hebrew for 'a Memorial and a Name') takes its title from Isaiah 56.5: 'And to them will I give in my house and within my walls a memorial and an everlasting name, imperishable for all time.' Non-Jews who risked or gave their lives to aid Jews in the Holocaust are listed as 'Righteous Among the Nations'. A tree, symbolizing the renewal of life, is planted and a plaque identifying the person is located beside it in the 'Garden of the Righteous': 'They are like trees planted by streams of water, which yield their fruit in its season, and their leaves do not wither' (Psalm 1.3, NRSV). The names of the 'Righteous' also appear on a 'Wall of Remembrance'.

---

9   Sidney G. Hall, *Christian Anti-Semitism and Paul's Theology*, Augsburg Fortress, Minneapolis, 1993.

Fewer than 20,000 names appear on the list authorized by Yad Vashem. The requirements set by Yad Vashem are explicit and simple: the 'Righteous' must have risked their lives in order to help Jews threatened by the Nazis, and must have done so without expectation of compensation or reward. By normal standards, the rescuers were not merely righteous but heroes; they acted beyond the call of duty. None of the principal religions has a *duty* of self-sacrifice, of acting heroically. Instead of asking, 'Why weren't there more helpers and rescuers?' we might well ask, 'How is it there were so many?' We are unlikely ever to find an adequate explanation for their extraordinary acts of conscience or courage.[10]

In the final analysis, helping Jews escape the Nazis was the exception. The historian Christopher Browning wrote, 'Ultimately, the Holocaust took place because at the most basic level individual human beings killed other human beings in large numbers over an extended period of time.' The individual acts of bravery, for instance of a Corrie ten Boom, of an Oskar Schindler, of the many brave Polish men and women hiding Jews and by Dutch citizens willing to hide and aid their fellow Jewish citizens, cannot obscure the fact that the vast majority opted for complicity with the Nazi genocide of the Jews, either by actively participating or by their indifference contributing to the ability of the Nazis so successfully to conduct their war against the Jews.

---

10 Berel Land, 'Undoing Certain Mischievous Questions about the Holocaust' in *Post Holocaust: Interpretation, misinterpretation and the claims of history*, Indiana University Press, Bloomington & Indianapolis, 2005, pp. 93–5.

The Nazi Holocaust:
a short timeline

Action is the only remedy to indifference:
the most insidious danger of all.
(Elie Wiesel, Nobel Peace Prize acceptance speech,
10 December 1986)

1933

30 January	Hitler becomes Chancellor of Germany
27 February	Reichstag fire, Berlin: many Communists and trade unionists arrested
22 March	Dachau, the first concentration camp, opens near Munich
1 April	Nazis stage national boycott of Jewish shops and businesses
	Jews excluded from civil service and teaching
26 April	Gestapo established by Herman Göring
10 May	Public burning of books by Jewish authors in Berlin and throughout Germany
14 July	Nazi Party only legal party in Germany
October	Germany withdraws from League of Nations

1934

30 June	'Night of the Long Knives': Hitler purges the *Sturmabteiling* (SA)

| 2 August | President Hindenburg dies. Hitler becomes Führer |

1935

| 16 March | Germany formally begins to rearm, violating Treaty of Versailles |
| 15 September | Nuremberg Laws deprive Jews of citizenship and right to hold public office |

1936

7 March	Germany reoccupies Rhineland, violating treaties
12 July	Sachsenhausen concentration camp opens outside Berlin
October	Hitler and Mussolini declare Rome–Berlin Axis
November	Japan and Germany make Anti-Comintern Pact

1937

| July | Buchenwald concentration camp opens near Weimar, Germany |

1938

| 12 March | Nazi troops enter Austria. Hitler announces *Anschluss* (union) with Austria All German anti-Semitic decrees applied in Austria |
| July | Evian Conference: American and European countries discuss German |

	Jewish refugee problem. Most countries refuse entry to Jewish refugees
1 August	Eichmann sets up Office of Jewish Emigration in Vienna to increase emigration
8 August	Himmler sets up Mauthausen concentration camp near Linz, Austria
30 September	Munich Crisis: Britain and France appease Hitler on Sudetenland to avoid war
October	Following request by Swiss, Germans mark Jewish passports with 'J' to prevent Jews emigrating to Switzerland
15 October	German troops occupy Sudetenland
6 November	Herschel Grynszpan shoots German diplomat in Paris to protest at German persecution of Jews
9/10 November	*Kristallnacht* pogrom. 91 Jews killed, 191 synagogues destroyed, 30,000 Jews sent to concentration camps
15 November	Jewish children excluded from non-Jewish German schools
3 December	Compulsory Aryanization of all Jewish businesses
	Emergency programme to evacuate Jewish children to Britain, France and Low Countries

1939

15 March	Germany occupies remainder of Czechoslovakia

28 March	Franco victorious in Spanish Civil War
18 May	Ravensbrück concentration camp opens in north Germany
23 August	Molotov–Ribbentrop Pact, non-aggression pact between Soviet Union and Germany. Secret agreement to divide Poland
1 September	Germany invades Poland
3 September	Great Britain and France declare war on Germany
October	Euthanasia programme starts in Germany: around 90,000 killed
26 October	Germany introduces forced labour for Polish Jews
23 November	All Jews in Poland to wear the Star of David

1940

12 February	First German Jews deported to Poland
30 April	Łódź ghetto, Poland, sealed off with 230,000 Jews inside
10 May	Germany invades France (350,000 Jews), Belgium (65,000 Jews), Netherlands (140,000 Jews) and Luxembourg (3,500 Jews)
	Winston Churchill becomes British Prime Minister
20 May	Auschwitz concentration camp set up, Poland
14 June	Germany occupies Paris
22 June	France surrenders to Germany

17 July	First anti-Jewish measures in Vichy (Southern) France
8 August	Battle of Britain begins
27 September	Tripartite (Axis) Pact signed by Germany, Italy and Japan
7 October	Germany invades Romania (34,000 Jews)
November	Hungary, Romania and Slovakia become German allies
15/16 November	500,000 Jews sealed up in Warsaw ghetto

1941

2 March	Germany occupies Bulgaria (50,000 Jews)
7 March	German Jews made to do forced labour
6 April	Germany invades Yugoslavia and Greece
21 April	Natzweiler-Struthof concentration camp opens in Alsace, France
May	3,600 Jews rounded up in Paris
22 June	Germany invades Soviet Union (3 million Jews)
	Einsatzgruppen (killing squads) murder Jews by shooting, gassing in vans and other means. Millions killed in Poland, Baltic states, western Soviet Union and Slavic states
21 July	Majdanek (Lublin) concentration camp opens, Poland
31 July	Göring gives Heydrich instructions for 'Final Solution'
17 September	General deportation of German Jews begins

19 September	All Jews in Reich must wear Star of David
28/29 September	*Einsatzcommando 4a* kill 33,771 Jews at Babi Yar, near Kiev
October	Auschwitz II (Birkenau) set up to exterminate Jews, Gypsies, Poles, Russians and others
2 October	German army starts drive on Moscow
23 October	Germany stops emigration of Jews
24 November	Terezín (Theresienstadt) concentration camp set up near Prague. Nazis use it as model for propaganda
7 December	Japan attacks Pearl Harbor, bringing USA into war
8 December	Chelmno, Poland, extermination camp starts operating
11/13 December	Germany and Italy declare war on USA

1942

January	Wannsee Conference, Berlin: Nazi leaders plan 'The Final Solution' – annihilation of European Jews
	Nazis start mass killing of Jews at Auschwitz-Birkenau
31 January	SS *Einsatzgruppe A* reports 229,052 Jews killed
	First transports to Belzec, Majdanek, Treblinka and Sobibór camps
24 March	Deportations of Slovakian Jews to Auschwitz begin

The Nazi Holocaust: a timeline

27 March	Deportations from France to Auschwitz begin
1 June	Jews in France, Holland, Belgium, Croatia, Slovakia, Romania to wear yellow star
2 July	Jews sent from Berlin to Terezín
7 July	Himmler permits sterilization experiments at Auschwitz
14 July	Germans start to deport Dutch Jews to Auschwitz
16/17 July	12,887 Paris Jews sent to Drancy internment camp
19 July	Operation Reinhard: mass deportation of Polish Jews to extermination camps
22 July	Deportations start from Warsaw ghetto to Treblinka
	Deportation of Belgian Jews to Auschwitz begins
August	World Jewish Congress tells Britain and USA of mass murder in eastern Europe
23 August	German army attacks Stalingrad
26/28 August	7,000 Jews in unoccupied (Vichy) France arrested
October	Allies win Second Battle of El Alamein
28 October	First transport from Terezín to Auschwitz
10 December	First transport of German Jews to Auschwitz
December	After murder of c. 600,000 Jews, exterminations at Belzec cease. Camp dismantled and ploughed over

1943

January	Battle of Stalingrad ends: Russia destroys German Sixth Army
29 January	Nazis plan to send all Gypsies to extermination camps
27 February	'Factory Action': Jewish workers in Berlin arms factories sent to Auschwitz
March	First crematorium opened at Auschwitz
14 March	Kraków ghetto liquidated
19 April	Warsaw ghetto rising begins when Germans try to liquidate 70,000 inhabitants
May	SS Dr Josef Mengele arrives at Auschwitz
19 May	Goebbels claims Berlin is *Judenfrei* (cleansed of Jews)
June	Lwów (Lemberg) ghetto liquidated
9/10 July	Allies invade Italy. Mussolini overthrown
11 September	Germany occupies Rome
14 October	Inmates revolt at Sobibór extermination camp
16 October	Jews in Rome rounded up: 1,000 sent to Auschwitz
December	Vilna (Vilnius) ghetto liquidated
2 December	First transport of Jews from Vienna arrives at Auschwitz

1944

19 March	Nazis occupy Hungary (725,000 Jews). Eichmann arrives with Gestapo

May–July	437,000 Hungarian Jews deported to Auschwitz; most gassed
June	Red Cross visits Terezín: makes favourable report
	Rome liberated
6 June	D-Day: Allies land in Normandy, France
20 July	German officers attempt to assassinate Hitler
24 July	Russian troops liberate Majdanek (Lublin) camp
4 August	Anne Frank and family sent to Auschwitz
6 August	Łódź (Litzmannstadt), last Jewish ghetto in Poland, liquidated
7 October	Revolt by inmates at Auschwitz; crematorium blown up
30 October	Last use of gas chambers at Auschwitz
November	Last Jews deported from Terezín to Auschwitz
8 November	'Death March': Germans make 25,000 Jews walk more than 100 miles from Budapest to Austrian border
25 November	Himmler orders destruction of crematoria at Auschwitz

1945

6 January	Red Army liberates Budapest
17 January	Red Army liberates Warsaw
27 January	Red Army liberates Auschwitz. About 2,000,000 people, including 1,500,000 Jews, had been murdered there

10 April	US army liberates Buchenwald
15 April	British Army liberates Bergen-Belsen concentration camp
23 April	Red Army reaches Berlin
29 April	US Seventh Army liberates Dachau
30 April	Hitler commits suicide in Berlin bunker
2 May	Red Cross take over Terezín
5 May	Mauthausen liberated
7 May	Germany surrenders unconditionally at Rheims
8 May	VE Day. Third Reich ends
23 May	Himmler commits suicide
6 August	Atom bomb on Hiroshima
9 August	Atom bomb on Nagasaki
2 September	Japan surrenders; Second World War ends
20 November	Nuremberg International Military Tribunal opens

1946

11 March	Auschwitz Commandant Höss arrested
16 October	Göring commits suicide at Nuremberg
9 December	Twenty-three SS doctors and scientists tried at Nuremberg. Sixteen found guilty, seven hanged

1947

15 September	Twenty-one SS-*Einsatz* leaders tried at Nuremberg. Four executed

1960

11 May   Israeli secret service capture Adolf
                     Eichmann in Argentina

1961

11 April–
14 August   Eichmann tried in Jerusalem

1962

31 May   Eichmann hanged at Ramleh, Israel

1

A most unorthodox nun

MOTHER MARIA OF PARIS

Anthony Bloom (1914–2003), who later became Metropolitan Anthony of Sourozh, never forgot meeting Maria Skobtsova in Paris in the 1930s: 'I was simply staggered when I saw her for the first time in monastic clothes. I was walking along the Boulevard du Montparnasse and I saw, in front of a café, on the pavement, there was a table, on the table was a glass of beer and behind the glass was sitting a Russian nun in full monastic robes. I looked at her and decided that I would never go near that woman.'

Maria – also known as Mother Maria, and later as Saint Maria of Paris – was born Elizaveta Yurievna Pilenko in 1891. A Russian aristocrat, poet, Orthodox nun and member of the French Resistance, she died at Ravensbrück concentration camp in 1944. Married twice, divorced twice and with three children by two different men, in 1985 she was recognized by Israel's Yad Vashem as one of the Righteous Among the Nations, while in 2004 the Eastern Orthodox Church canonized her as a saint.

Elizaveta Pilenko was born into an aristocratic and devoutly Orthodox Christian family in Riga, Latvia, at that time part of the Russian Empire, though they originated in Anapa, Ukraine, on the shores of the Black Sea. While she was still in her teens, Liza's father died, a loss that hit her hard and led her temporarily to turn her back on Christianity. In rebellion she wrote, 'This death is not useful to anybody. It is unjust therefore there is no justice. But if there is no justice there cannot be a just God. If there is no just God then there is no God at all!'

In 1906 Liza's mother, Sophia née Delaunay – a descendant of the last governor of the Paris Bastille, destroyed in 1789 – moved to St Petersburg, where Liza encountered for the first time, and was lastingly influenced by, both the urban poor and radical intellectuals. She published a book of poems, and in 1910 married in haste a young Bolshevik law student named Dmitriy Kuz'min-Karavaev. They soon parted.

Gradually Elizaveta turned back to Christianity, becoming the first woman to enrol at the Theological Academy of the Alexander Nevsky Monastery in St Petersburg – although she was allowed to study only at home. In 1918, following the cataclysm of the October Revolution, Liza was appointed mayor of Anapa. Accused by White Russians of being a Bolshevik, she was put on trial, acquitted, and then fell in love with and married the trial judge, Danilo Skobtsov, a former teacher.

The 1917 Revolution and ensuing civil war uprooted many Russians, more than a million of whom fled into exile in Europe, many of them to France. In 1923, amid the continuing chaos, Liza, Danilo, her daughter Gaiana, son Yuri and mother Sophia all fled via Constantinople (Istanbul) to Paris, where they joined the burgeoning community of Russian émigrés attempting to sustain a living.

In Paris, Liza scraped an existence by sewing, making dolls and painting silk scarves. When her daughter Anastasia ('Nastia'), who had been born in Yugoslavia during the family's travels, died of meningitis, Liza experienced a religious and emotional crisis that led her to believe God was calling her to serve the poor and outcast among the Russian émigrés. 'I never knew the meaning of repentance, but now I am aghast at my own insignificance,' she wrote. 'At Nastia's side I feel that my soul has meandered down back-alleys all my life. And now I want an authentic and a purified road, not out of faith in life, but in order to justify, understand and accept death.' Maria saw 'a new road before [her] and a new meaning to life, to be a mother for all, for all who need maternal care, assistance or protection.' Since she could no longer be mother to her daughter, she decided she would be mother to everyone she encountered. 'There are no words greater than these three: "Love one another,"' she wrote. 'Believe in these words, then all life will be justified and illuminated.'

To accomplish these new goals, she decided she would take vows as a nun – somewhat problematic for a twice-married, 40-year-old mother of three. Scandalizing a large section of the Russian diaspora, the head of the Orthodox Church in Europe, Russian Orthodox bishop Metropolitan Evlogy Georgievsky (1868–1946), suggested that Liza should become a 'revolutionary nun'. She followed his proposal, taking the veil yet staying in the world. She did, however, decide to separate from her husband, Danilo, then working as a Paris taxi driver. Adopting the name 'Maria', Liza took vows in 1932, with the proviso that she would not live in monastic seclusion but be permitted to follow a 'monasticism in the world'. 'Take me,

I am your stone,' she implored in a poem; 'build with me, inscrutable Architect.' So began a nun's life that shocked some, but saved many others.

As travelling secretary for the Russian Student Christian Mission, Maria now journeyed widely in Western Europe, visiting and speaking to Russian emigrants scraping an existence in the slums of cities such as Marseilles, southern France, many of them addicted to drugs and alcohol. Then, over the next ten years, Mother Maria set up a number of homes in and near Paris as havens for the destitute.

In December 1932, with no money to her name, but a gift of 5,000 francs from Metropolitan Evlogy, Maria rented the first of these houses, a two-storey building at 9 villa de Saxe, in Paris's relatively prosperous 7th arrondissement, not far from Les Invalides. There was no furniture apart from a piano – but Maria had no interest in music. This centre was soon equipped as a place of respite and refuge for people in need, largely young Russian women. Maria gathered a little community of co-workers, who turned an upstairs room into a chapel for which Mother Maria painted the iconostasis, the screen separating the nave from the sanctuary in an Orthodox church. When the numbers at this house grew, Maria gave up her own room, opting to sleep in the basement. 'She is tucked into a little corner behind the boiler,' noted a friend. 'A narrow iron bedstead; a hole in the floor, stuffed with an old boot: a rat lives there.'

A typical day for Mother Maria began early with a journey to Les Halles, the central Paris fruit and vegetable market, to beg for unwanted food or bargain for cheap provisions. The nun soon became a well-known figure: dressed shabbily, often in worn men's boots and a stained second-hand cassock, with a cigarette hanging from her lips. She would return to her community on the Métro, carrying on her back a sack of bones, fish and overripe fruit and vegetables. At the house, free soup and hot meals were constantly available for street-sleepers and vagrants. The work she carried out was not dissimilar to that of the Salvation Army.

The community grew fast and was soon feeding as many as one hundred people every day. When the first house became too small, the community relocated in 1934 to larger premises in the 15th arrondissement, close to the Seine, an area inhabited by many impoverished Russian refugees. Their new double-fronted, three-storey building at 77 rue de Lourmel had been left unoccupied since the First World War. Maria described the 18-roomed house graphically:

> The house is roomy, but dusty, grubby, humble and unattractive; yet it is redeemed by its warm sense of shelter, security and gratifying huddling together in this redemptive Noah's Ark, which has nothing to fear from the waves of life's threatening elements, from the horror of rent overdue, of the impoverishment and despair of unemployment. Here people can wait awhile, regain their breath and gain temporary shelter until the time comes to stand on their own two feet again.

By 1937 the community was housing several dozen women guests and serving up to 120 dinners daily, charging the unemployed a mere two francs. 'Some pay their way, while others find it impossible to contribute even half their dues,' said Maria. '[Others] earn their keep by some form of work.'

**77 rue de Lourmel, where Mother Maria housed
many unemployed people and refugees**

Over time, the community rented additional houses: a large house for families in need at 43 rue François Gerard in the 16th arrondissement; humbler premises for single men at 74 rue Felix Fauré, in the 15th; and a larger rural property mainly for people suffering from tuberculosis – and later for old people – at Noisy-le-Grand, about 18 miles east of Paris, with a converted henhouse for a chapel. Thousands eventually passed through these homes, finding rest and healing, and staying as long as necessary.

Mother Maria never doubted she was doing God's will. 'At the Last Judgment, I shall not be asked whether I practised asceticism satisfactorily, nor how many bows I made before the divine altar,' she wrote. 'Instead I shall be asked whether I fed the hungry, clothed the naked, visited the sick and the prisoner in his jail.' Sometimes she disappeared for days on end, seeking the homeless, sharing their existence and inviting them back to rue de Lourmel for an inexpensive meal and companionship. 'My feeling for them all is maternal,' she said. 'I would like to swaddle them and rock them to sleep.' And elsewhere: 'It is better to be a hysterical beggar woman or God's fool than to sit and drink tea and eat holy bread.'

Feeling a compulsion to help her guests, she often absented herself from services: 'Piety, piety,' she wrote in her journal, '– but where is the love that moves mountains?'

A serious multitasker, Mother Maria combined a number of roles: nun, counsellor, administrator, fundraiser, cook, poet, mother and organizer. Many were scandalized by this shabby nun, so uncompromising in her hospitality. 'For many in church circles we are too far to the left,' she declared, 'while for the left we are too church-minded.' Plenty of the Russian émigrés were outraged by her unconventional behaviour and appearance: she was much too casual about church ritual, she smoked and drank, she befriended the most objectionable people. For Maria, this echoed powerfully criticism levelled at Jesus by the religious leaders of his day, and thus justified her mission.

During the 'phoney war' after the commencement of the Second World War in September 1939, commodities became

Mother Maria at Lourmel, Paris

scarcer and food less available at Les Halles. Poverty and hunger increased, and in response the Paris *mairie* opened municipal canteens to provide food for the needy. In the summer of 1940, rue de Lourmel was renamed *Cantine Municipale* No. 9 and became an official food distribution centre, serving both Russian émigrés and poor Parisians.

On 14 June 1940 Paris fell to the Germans. Instantly, life changed for the worse. More than two-thirds of the city's population fled southwards, at least temporarily. Those who remained lived under increasingly rigorous Nazi control. 'If the Germans take Paris, I shall stay here with my old women,' Maria had declared. 'Where else could I send them?' Yet she had no illusions about Nazism. 'The master race,' she opined, was 'led by a madman who needs a strait-jacket and should be placed in a cork-lined room so that his bestial wailing will not disturb the world at large.' She faced the future with equanimity. 'If the worst comes to the worst,' she wrote bravely to friends, 'the Germans will shut me up in a concentration camp. Yet people live on even in the camps.'

The Russian refugees were among the first targets of the Nazi occupying forces. In June 1941, after Germany suddenly attacked Communist Russia, one thousand Russians in Paris, among them several of Maria's friends, were arrested and interned at Royallieu-Compiègne internment and deportation camp (*Frontstalag* 122), north-east of Paris. She quickly threw in her lot with the Resistance, making contact with the Catholic underground movement led by the Jesuit Father Pierre Chaillet (1900–72) and launching an aid project for the prisoners and their dependents.

At greatest risk were the Jews who had also been taken to Compiègne, prior to being transported to Auschwitz. Hearing from Russian internees that the Jews were being singled out for barbaric treatment, Mother Maria and colleagues at Lourmel worked with the Resistance to aid them, collecting food and smuggling it into the camp.

Mother Maria regarded an attack on the Jews as an attack on the image of God in all men and women. To defend the Jews, she believed, was to defend all of humanity, all that makes us human. She saw the persecution of the Jews as a challenge to all that Christians held dear: 'There is no such thing as a Christian problem. Don't you realize the battle is being waged against Christianity? . . . The age of confessors [that is, Christians who suffer persecution for their faith] has arrived. The majority will fall to temptation. But the Saviour said, "Fear not, little flock".'

In December 1941, in dark days of the war, she wrote a hopeful verse paraphrase of Isaiah 21.11–12:

At night a starless sky.
A distant dog, a bark.
Now the watchman sounds his warning.
Time for thieves to be about.

'Watchman, is it long till dawn?'
His voice comes from the dark:
'It's still night, but nearly morning.
Morning's coming, never doubt.'

Around this time a huge redhead named George Reyevski, every inch the romantic poet, found refuge at Lourmel. A Russian Jew, he had been baptized years earlier and convinced himself this was sufficient to keep him safe from the Nazis. Mother Maria eventually persuaded him otherwise and induced him to move south to Burgundy, outside the German-occupied zone, where he found work as a tutor and survived the war.

Father Dimitri Klepinin (1904–44), a mild, sensitive, calm and self-effacing Orthodox priest, had arrived at Lourmel to help on 10 October 1939. Completely different in temperament from Maria, quite newly ordained and with a scholarly back-ground, he was nevertheless prepared to deceive and lie to the Nazis as and when necessary.

Early in 1942, the Nazi administration announced that every Jew in France must be registered. Immediately many from the Jewish community began to ask Father Dimitri to issue them with a baptismal certificate that would help them claim Christian status. The priest supplied dozens of 'mercy baptisms', putting his own life in constant jeopardy. Those who genuinely wanted to become Christians he baptized. To the rest, he simply gave a baptismal card, with his wife Tamara or sister Tanya serving as godmother in many instances. 'I think the good Christ would give me this paper if I were in their place,' he said. 'So I must do it.' To cover his tracks, he entered the Jews' names in his registers, listing them as members of the Lourmel congre-gation, in case the French police or Nazi officials checked the certificates' authenticity. He even took photographs of those he supplied with baptismal certificates and learned their names by heart so that he could vouch for them. His records survive, with around 80 names marked with a 't' to denote 'false' baptism.

When a probing diocesan administrator asked for details of his baptismal activities, Dimitri replied evasively, 'In answer to your request that I submit a list of those newly baptized since 1940, I take the liberty of stating that all those who, regardless of external circumstances, have received baptism at my hands are by the same token my spiritual children and under my immediate care. Your request could only have been provoked by external pressure and dictated to you by consideration of public order. In view of this I am obliged to withhold the information requested.' The church official failed to recognize and adapt to the critical pressures and threats of the perilous times, preferring to stick with bureaucratic and ecclesiastical tradition.

In March 1942, Adolf Eichmann ordered all Jews aged six and above in German-occupied territories to wear the yellow Star of David on their outer clothing. From 7 June 1942, this order was enforced in occupied France. The same day, Maria wrote a poem entitled 'Israel', which opens and closes with the following verses (of which there are several versions):

Two triangles, King David's star.
No insult, this ancestral badge.
It indicates a noble way.
It marks a chosen nation.

May you, stamped by this seal,
this star of David, by decree,
in your constrained response reveal
that you are spiritually free.

Many Christians said that Eichmann's new regulation had nothing to do with them, so did not present a problem. 'If we were true Christians we would all wear the star,' Maria responded spiritedly. 'You are persecuted again, O Israel. But what can human ill-will mean to you, who have heard the thunder from Sinai?'

For the Jews, further restrictions soon followed. From July 1942, Jews were banned from parks, theatres and cinemas, cafés and restaurants, swimming pools, racecourses and campsites, museums and libraries. They could travel only at limited, inconvenient hours and occupy only the last carriage of railway trains. They were not permitted to use the main streets or to leave home after 8 p.m. Jews were barred from almost all public places and could shop for only one hour a day. In effect, they became invisible in public.

Maria was particularly exercised that Jewish children couldn't spend time in public parks. 'To forbid little children the sun, the sky and the air! I feel a great anger,' she told friends, so she took a little group to play in a garden where a retired Jewish man sat smoking his pipe. 'I can mind the children, Mother,' he told her. 'You have more important things to do.' So he sat with his old raincoat pulled tight to hide his yellow star, until he was arrested the following month.

Maria and Dimitri now began to work with the Resistance to conceal fugitives and feed them into the network facilitating escape to the south of France, which had not as yet been occupied by Nazi Germany. It was a complex and dangerous activity for which they needed to provide forged documents for the fugitives. Closed down the previous year, Maria's house at Noisy now came into its own as a secret refuge for Jews and members of the Resistance.

Astonishingly, some at Lourmel still failed to recognize the gravity of their situation, insisting they were safe as long as their papers were in order. Sometimes Mother Maria's own excitable, extravagant personality even threatened the safety of the Lourmel community. In an otherwise innocuous phone conversation, she blurted out to a priest, 'I'm hiding Jews!' and when the first escaped Russian prisoner of war arrived, she insisted on introducing him publicly to everybody present. The anti-Semitic views of some Russian émigrés also caused problems for Mother Maria and Father Dimitri, not to mention the frightened fugitives.

On 15 and 16 July 1942 the mass arrest of the Jews of Paris began. The authorities issued 28,000 arrest warrants, one for every Jewish person aged between 2 and 60; 12,884 people were successfully rounded up. Of these, 6,900 were first taken to the Vélodrome d'Hiver stadium – the 'Vél d'Hiv', near the Eiffel Tower, less than a mile from rue de Lourmel – the rest to Drancy internment and transportation centre in north-east Paris. Dorothée and Samuel Epstein described conditions at Drancy in a letter to their daughter Nathalie:

Filth of a coal mine. Straw mattress full of lice and bedbugs. Horrid overcrowding. Eighty-six women, six water taps, you don't have time to wash. There are paralyzed women, women who have had breast operations and can't move their arms, pregnant women, blind women, deaf mutes, women on stretchers, women who have left their small children all alone. Old women of sixty-three. You can't go to the toilet more than once every sixteen hours.

Of those confined at the Vél d'Hiv, 4,051 were mere children. Within five days they were to be separated from their parents and sent to Auschwitz via Drancy. This erstwhile cycling stadium was poorly ventilated and in the midsummer sun became stiflingly hot beneath its blue-painted glass roof. The internees had to sleep on the ground or on terraced benches. The toilets were completely blocked so people relieved themselves publicly in corners, creating a degrading stench amid the pervading noise and chaos. One observer said there was 'no trace of even the slightest organisation, no direction, no one in charge'.

Hearing that two priests had gained access to the arena, Mother Maria boldly went to see if she could do anything to help, dressed for once in a clean robe and her distinctive nun's *klobuk* headdress. She persuaded a French guard to admit her to the compound, where she found just ten toilets and a single water hydrant – and even that was cut off. The terrified crowd massed into the arena included patients dragged from hospital, the mentally ill, young mothers and infants, children with infectious diseases and people on stretchers. Many of the children were completely alone, lacking any adult care or protection. Some were put to death by their parents, to avoid the horrors they foresaw.

On 31 July and the days following, nine trains left Paris, transporting 9,000 adults and older children to Auschwitz; 3,500 children aged under 14 remained in the velodrome with neither parents nor older siblings until August, when they too were transported to Auschwitz. None returned.

For three days Mother Maria did what she could to help, distributing the small amounts of food she was able to take in with her. She even managed to rescue a few children, helped by refuse collectors who smuggled them out inside rubbish bins. At least two boys and a little girl were saved in this way.

Meanwhile the house at rue de Lourmel was full to bursting with people, many of them Jews. 'Lourmel is overcrowded,' wrote Mother Maria. 'There are people in the wing and in the shed; there are people sleeping on the refectory floor. A whole family is sheltering in Father Dimitri's room; another in Yuri's. Both Jews and non-Jews.' Local resistance workers helped supply food for the community. 'I was able to supply Mother Maria with bread, ration-cards, flour, groats and other products . . . ,' one reported.

Mother Maria managed to provide some of the Jewish fugitives with false Aryan documents, removing or concealing their yellow stars, and sending them on to another place of refuge. Often she didn't tell even her closest co-workers where the guests were going – in many instances Catholic monasteries and convents. 'It's amazing that the Germans haven't yet pounced on us,' she exclaimed. 'If the Germans do come to Lourmel, I'll show them the icon of the Mother of God.'

'The Mother of God might be all right,' commented one resident, 'but live Jews would present more of a problem.' We will never know exactly how many Jews found refuge at Lourmel and its associated houses, where Maria and her team did all they could to conceal and protect them.

When the Nazis pasted up posters at Lourmel calling for Frenchmen to work in German factories, Maria immediately ripped them down. A German pastor arrived at Lourmel, claiming he was interested in Mother Maria's Christian social work. She quickly deduced that he belonged to the Nazified *Deutsche Christen* ('German Christians', a movement within the German Evangelical Church that wanted to purge the

Gospels of non-Aryan themes). 'How can you be a Christian *and* a Nazi?' she demanded.

After Christmas 1942 rumours became rife that the Gestapo and the SD (*Sicherheitsdienst* – the Reich Security Service) were watching Mother Maria and Father Dimitri. Both had been denounced for aiding Jews and were liable to be arrested. The previous August they had been interrogated by Hans Hoffmann, an SD officer from the Paris Gestapo headquarters in the rue des Saussaies, opposite the Elysée Palace. The Gestapo were building up a dossier on the activities at Lourmel but had as yet found nothing sufficiently incriminating to arrest them. Friends pressed both of them to go underground.

On 8 February 1943 Hoffmann came to Lourmel accompanied by two black-uniformed Gestapo agents. When he was told Maria wasn't there, he started to search the building and seized her files. Maria's son Yuri acted quickly, setting fire to some compromising documents, such as anti-Nazi pamphlets and resistance publications, and hiding others with cash in the crib of Klepinin's young son, Paul. He then attempted to escape so he could warn his mother, but Hoffmann noticed him. When he was searched, the Germans found in Yuri's pocket a letter in Russian to Father Dimitri from a Jewish woman named Gavronskaia,[1] requesting a baptismal certificate. Hoffmann, whose second language was Russian, realized immediately what the priest had been doing. He took Yuri back to the Gestapo HQ as a hostage, hoping this would induce Maria to return. When Mother Maria heard her son was being held by Hoffmann, she took the train to Paris and gave herself up. After

---

1 This woman later died in Auschwitz.

interrogation, release and re-arrest, Maria realized Hoffmann had in his possession ample incriminating documents and denunciations, so she admitted to everything.

'You brought your daughter up badly!' Hoffmann taunted Maria's 80-year-old mother, Sophia. 'All she does is help Jews!'

The old lady responded, 'My daughter is a real Christian . . . For her there is neither Greek nor Jew.[2] If you had been in trouble, she would have helped you too.' Hoffmann warned that Sophia would never see her daughter again.

The Gestapo interrogated Father Dimitri for four hours at rue des Saussaies. He made no attempt to be evasive and told Hoffmann exactly what he had been doing, but stressed that Maria's son Yuri 'had no part in it'. Hoffmann offered the priest freedom if he agreed to stop helping the Jews. Dimitri pledged that he would carry on his work if released: 'I am a Christian and act as I must.' Hoffmann denounced him as a 'Jew-lover'. 'How dare you speak of helping these pigs as a Christian duty,' he yelled, and hit the priest across the face. Father Dimitri raised his pectoral cross and asked the Nazi, 'This Jew here, do you know him?' This time he was knocked to the floor.

Maria, her son Yuri and Father Dimitri were all now taken from Gestapo HQ to the Fort de Romainville internment and transit camp at Les Lilas, Paris. On 27 February Dimitri and Yuri were transferred via rue des Saussaies to the Royallieu-Compiègne internment camp. The house at Lourmel was shut down.[3]

---

2 'There is neither Jew nor Greek, there is neither slave nor free, there is neither male nor female; for you are all one in Christ Jesus.' Galatians 3.28, NKJV.

3 The building survived to the 1960s, when it was demolished and flats were built on the site.

The Compiègne camp was operated by the Germans and divided by barbed wire into three separate sections: one for French Communists, another for Russian prisoners of war and the third for Jews. There was no furniture, running water, heating or electricity. 'About 400 of us were assembled in the yard . . . Father Dimitri, his cassock torn, was made a laughing-stock. One of the SS began to prod and beat him, calling him *Jude* [Jew]. Yuri Skobtsov, who was standing beside him, was in tears. Father Dimitri started to comfort him, saying Christ withstood greater mockery than this.'

Maria was later also taken to Compiègne, where she saw her son Yuri for the last time. Then, on 21 April 1943, Maria and 200 other women were locked into cattle trucks to make the long journey east on Transport 19,000. Yuri wrote to their friends at Lourmel:

> My most dear and precious ones, you probably know already that I saw mama on the night of her departure for Germany, she was in a remarkable state of mind and told me . . . that I must trust in her ability to bear things and in general not to worry about her. Every day we remember her at the *proskomedia*[4] (and you as well). We celebrate the Eucharist and receive communion each day.

Maria and her fellow prisoners were confined in the railway trucks for three days with neither sanitation nor water. At last they arrived at Fürstenberg station, Mecklenburg, the infamous alighting point for Ravensbrück concentration camp,

---

4 The act of preparing the bread and wine for the Eucharist.

where Maria was to spend her next two years as a Nazi prisoner, tattooed with the numerals 19263.

Yuri and Father Dimitri remained at Compiègne until 16 December 1943. Dimitri was able to improvise a church where Orthodox and Catholic services were held on alternate days. However, in January 1944, Yuri and Dimitri were transferred to Buchenwald concentration camp, near Weimar. Just before they left, Yuri sent a letter of astonishing maturity and courage to his friends at Lourmel:

I am to go to Germany . . . I am absolutely calm, even somewhat proud to share mama's fate. I promise you I will bear everything with dignity. Whatever happens, sooner or later, we shall all be together. I can say in all honesty that I am not afraid of anything any more: my chief anxiety is you, I would be thoroughly content if I could leave in the awareness that you are calm and that you possess that peace of which no powers can ever deprive us. I ask anyone whom I have hurt in any way to forgive me. Christ be with you!

As soon as they arrived at the camp, their heads were shaved and they were given the now so familiar striped prison uniforms. They were then transported a further 40 kilometres to Dora camp, where they joined forced labour gangs building the tunnels where parts for V1 and V2 weapons were to be constructed. The death toll at Dora was appallingly high.

Within ten days, Yuri's body erupted in boils. He was suffering from furunculosis, a disease caused by the atrocious living conditions, and which can quickly lead to septicaemia.

The Nazis made no attempt to treat him. On 6 February 1944, 24-year-old Yuri, prisoner 38893, was 'dispatched for treatment' – a sick euphemism for extermination. Four days later Father Dimitri also died, on the dirt floor of the camp hut, suffering from pneumonia. His body was disposed of in the Buchenwald crematorium on 10 February.

Mother Maria soon became the same beacon of hope at Ravensbrück 'model re-education camp' that she had been in Paris. Stripped of her nun's habit, showered and shaved, she was initially quarantined in Block 5 before being assigned to Block 27, at the south-west corner of the camp. Women prisoners were given a simple shift, long knickers, a blue-striped dress and white headdress. If they washed their clothes, the only way of drying them was to hang them damp over their arms.

Maria was able to contact prisoners in other barracks, and particularly in Block 31, where many Soviet prisoners were housed. Some Ravensbrück prisoners were made to work at the nearby Siemens-Halske factory, but Russian prisoners had to work in fields outside the camp. When they returned at the end of the day they sometimes brought Maria a potato or carrot they had managed to smuggle back, food which Maria often shared with other prisoners in particular need. Apart from this the only food was thin soup, served morning and evening.

In the midst of this horror, Maria organized evening prayers in the barrack room, reading to fellow prisoners from the Gospels: 'Mother Maria would pick up a Christian handbook that one of the prisoners had managed to retain when she was searched, and read a passage from the Gospels and the Epistles. We would comment on the texts and meditate on them. Often we would finish with Compline.'[5] Although Maria 'prayed with believers and read the Gospels [with them]', noted another prisoner, 'she never preached [to non-believers] but discussed religion [solely] with those who wanted to . . . Wherever and however she could, she would sustain the as yet incompletely extinguished flame of humanity.'

'I don't know what Mother Maria said to them,' a fellow prisoner named Rosane Lascroux remembered, 'but they would go off radiant. When they came to her oppressed, she comforted them and embraced them like children.' A Jewish mother went to Mother Maria to tell her she was to be sent to Auschwitz with her two children the following day. 'Mother, I can't bear it. What shall I do?' she wept. Maria embraced the woman, also weeping.

'Can I ask you to be brave in the face of senseless hatred?' she asked. 'Or to go to that place with your children with a joyful heart? I can't, because I don't believe you should. But I tell you with all my heart that, were it possible, I would go in your place . . . You will not be forgotten.'

Eventually, late in 1943, friends in Paris discovered where Maria was being held and sent her food parcels and letters. She even received a final message from her son, Yuri.

At Easter 1944 Maria reportedly decorated some of the windows of her block with decoupage of white paper: 'Christ is risen!' she told her fellow Russian prisoners. Extraordinary as it might seem, Mother Maria even managed to do some embroidery in this death camp. The only piece that survived was an

---

5 The traditional service for the end of the day.

image of the Allied invasion of Normandy, based on the Bayeux Tapestry. Sewing materials were hard to come by: 'The colours were obtained by a Polish friend, who worked on the dyeing of SS shirts. The threads were derived from the insulation of electric flexes, which were cut and bared by the camp's Siemens machinery. The needle was stolen from the tailoring workshop . . . Fellow prisoners brought all these for the embroidery, at the risk of their lives.'

Mother Maria took particular care of younger women prisoners. 'She took us under her wing . . . She was full of good cheer, really good cheer. We had roll-calls which lasted a great deal of time. We were woken at three in the morning and had to stand out in the open in the middle of winter until all the barracks were counted. She took all this calmly and would say, "Well that's that, yet another day completed. And tomorrow it will be the same all over again. But one fine day the time will come for all of this to end."'

A fellow prisoner named Solange Perichon remembered:

She was never downcast, never. She never complained . . . She was on good terms with everyone. Anyone in the block, no matter who it was, knew her on equal terms. She was the kind of person who made no distinction between people [whether they] held extremely progressive political views [or had] religious beliefs radically different from her own. She allowed nothing of secondary importance to impede her contact with people.

Another prisoner, Sophia Nosovich, once confided to Maria that she was 'ceasing to feel anything whatsoever. My very thought processes were numbed and had ground to a halt. "No, no," Mother Maria responded, "whatever you do, continue to think. In the conflict with doubt, cast your thought wider and deeper. Let it transcend the conditions and limitations of this earth.'"

At first it seemed as if death was not imminent for Mother Maria. A postcard from her arrived in Paris on 28 January 1944: 'I am strong and healthy,' she wrote in German, but added in Russian, 'I have altogether become an old woman.' She conserved her energy as best she could. Sometimes she was able to work in the knitwear workshop, where it was less tedious and exhausting, and the threat to health lower than for work parties in the forests and marshes surrounding the camp. There were even times when – without the guards' knowledge – she stayed in the dormitory block and did no work.

Some have suggested that Mother Maria's rigorous form of life as a nun, with its lack of privacy or personal security, helped her to survive the concentration camp longer than some others. Whether or not that is the case, overcrowding, heavy work, disease and malnutrition eventually took their toll. By late 1944 Maria was so seriously ill that she decided to accept the pink card offered by the camp authorities to those who were unfit for work or aged over 65. After 15 January 1945 prisoners holding such cards, including Mother Maria, were transported to the *Jugendlager*, a camp adjoining Ravensbrück, intended to expedite their death.

By this time the Nazis had realized that they were losing the war and planned to kill as many prisoners as possible before the end. Food in the *Jugendlager* was rationed to less than half that at Ravensbrück: the bread ration was reduced

**Monument by Horst J. Meuter commemorating the victims of
Ravensbrück, in Brussels, Belgium**
Wiki commons

from 150 grams to 60 grams, accompanied by half a ladle of thin soup. Although winter temperatures dropped as low as −26 ºC, blankets, coats and jackets were confiscated, and later shoes and stockings, in an inhuman attempt to speed death. On average, 50 prisoners perished every day. Maria survived five weeks at the new camp, though suffering from severe dysentery. Then, incomprehensibly, she was transferred back to the main camp.

By March 1945, however, Maria was so weak that she had to lie down between roll-calls. 'What funny legs I have now!' she said to a fellow prisoner, Jacqueline Pery. 'Long and skinny, like an urchin – all knees.' But by now she scarcely spoke. 'Her face revealed intense inner suffering,' recalled Pery. 'Already it bore the marks of death. Nevertheless, Mother Maria made no complaint. She kept her eyes closed and seemed to be in a state of continual prayer.'

Concealed by friends in the space between the ceiling of the barrack room and the roof, she twice survived selection for dispatch back to the *Jugendlager* and certain death. However, on Good Friday, 30 March 1945, she was unable to rise. Maria's glasses were removed and she was taken to the gas chamber. Some say she was selected to die, others that she took the place of another prisoner. 'It's completely possible she took the place of a frantic companion,' reported Jacqueline Pery. 'That would have been entirely in keeping with her generous life.'

Mother Maria died the following day, Holy Saturday, when Orthodox Christians mark Christ's rest in the tomb. By this time the shellfire of the approaching Red Army could be heard inside the camp, and the International Red Cross had already evacuated hundreds of French and Norwegian women prisoners. Red Cross officials were waiting at the camp gates, but the camp commander told them he wasn't 'available'.

In 1985 Yad Vashem listed both Mother Maria and Father Dimitri as Righteous Gentiles. No one knows how many lives they saved. In 2004, at the Cathedral of St Alexander Nevsky, Paris, the Ecumenical Patriarchate canonized Mother Maria as a saint, along with her son Yuri and Father Dimitri Klepinin. According to Metropolitan Anthony of Sourozh, 'Mother Maria is a saint of our day and for our day; a woman of flesh and blood possessed by the love of God, who stood face to face with the problems of [the twentieth] century.'

2

Pestilent priests

THE REVD HUGH GRIMES AND THE REVD FREDERICK COLLARD, VIENNA

Vienna was not a good place to be a Jew in 1938. It hadn't been for a long time. Anti-Semitism was already common in the nineteenth-century capital of the crumbling Austro-Hungarian Empire. The founder of psychoanalysis, Sigmund Freud, recalled his childhood shock when his father was jostled and mocked in the street for being a Jew. The great symphonic composer, the Jewish Gustav Mahler, could be appointed conductor of the *Wiener Hofoper* (Vienna Court Opera) only after he had been baptized into the dominant Roman Catholic Church. Many assimilated and educated Jews in Vienna entered as fully as possible into the cultural and political life of the city, being baptized partly in order to circumvent laws that restricted Jewish access to important positions in public life, such as the Austrian civil service, the judiciary and medicine.

In the late nineteenth and early twentieth centuries, many Jews fleeing pogroms and conflict in Poland and Russia – *Ostjuden* (eastern Jews) – had settled in Vienna. Distinctive with their traditional black kaftans, broad-brimmed hats and long beards, they were resented and despised alike by Gentiles and many assimilated Austrian Jews.

Following the Allied victory in the First World War, the extensive Austro-Hungarian Empire shrank into the geographically small and politically unstable Austrian Republic. With the dismantling of the imperial aristocracy, much of the political and social leadership it had provided was taken on by Jews. Many in the German-speaking nations scapegoated the Jews and Communists for their defeat in the First World War and the ensuing economic and political problems. Anti-Semitic restrictions, oppression and violence became rife.

By March 1938, 185,028 Jews were recorded as living in Austria, the great majority in the capital, Vienna, the most Jewish city in the German-speaking world. In a city boasting as many as 94 synagogues and 120 Jewish welfare organizations, almost 10 per cent of the population was Jewish, totalling 176,034.

The Revd Hugh Grimes (1875–1962) was appointed chaplain of Christ Church, the little Anglican chapel in Jaurèsgasse attached to the British Embassy, in November 1934. Charles Hugh Duffy Grimes, to give him his full name, had been educated at Jesus College, Cambridge, before being ordained as a priest at St Albans, Hertfordshire, in 1904. From 1907, Grimes taught history in Australia for 12 years, and then returned to a parish post in England, where in 1924 he gained a fellowship in the Royal Geographical Society for his Church Army-sponsored research into migration. Grimes seems to have become habituated to travel and now took on a succession of chaplaincy positions in Europe – in Barcelona,

Le Havre and Biarritz – before arriving in Vienna in 1934.[1]
It has been claimed that Grimes was not only an Anglican
clergyman but also an employee of the SIS (MI6) – the British
Secret Intelligence Service.[2]

Under the imperial protocols of 1874, within Vienna only
the Roman Catholic rite was permitted, apart from Protestant
worship according to the Lutheran Augsburg Confession or
the Calvinist Helvetic Confession. In addition, the officiating
priest had always to be an Austrian subject. When the British
Ambassador objected to these conditions, the Austrian
government relented sufficiently to allow the building of a small
Anglican church, under the protection and jurisdiction of the
British Embassy, which was opened in 1877. The church seated
fewer than 150 people and served mainly embassy staff and
expatriates living and working in Vienna.

Soon after he arrived in Vienna, Revd Grimes became
friendly with several leading families in the city's Jewish
community. He visited neighbouring Germany in October
1935, just after the anti-Semitic and racial Nuremberg Laws
had been instigated, prohibiting marriage and extramarital
sexual intercourse between Jews and Germans, and depriving
those not of 'German or related blood' of citizenship rights –
classing them as mere 'state subjects'. The *Blutschutzgesetz* ('law
for the protection of blood') prohibited the use of the word
konfessionslos ('no denomination') on birth certificates: Jews
who no longer practised or identified with the Jewish faith were

---

1 It is a pity that in his popular book *A Field Guide to the English Clergy* (OneWorld,
   London, 2018), Fergus Butler-Gallie treats Hugh Grimes rather facetiously.

2 Helen Fry, *Spymaster: The secret life of Kendrick*, CreateSpace, Scotts Valley, CA,
   2014, p. 171.

**Christ Church, Vienna, where the Revd Hugh Grimes
and the Revd Frederick Collard served as chaplain**
Wiki commons: Claus Rainer Michalek

still required to identify themselves as 'Jewish'. This legislation had a devastating social and economic impact upon German Jews, but as yet the largely assimilated Jewish community did not for the most part recognize the threat posed by Hitler and the Nazi Party's race-based anti-Semitism.

Grimes was clearly aware of Austrian anti-Semitism from early in the 1930s. In a letter to George Bell, the Bishop of Chichester,[3] who as early as 1933 had warned publicly about the Nazis' anti-Semitic activities, Revd Grimes wrote, 'I may say that I myself am pro-Jew and have always been so.' He also told the bishop that he thought Britain and the USA should ask Germany to cease oppressing the Jews: 'Obviously such declarations need to be conveyed to the government as wisely as possible, otherwise they will only strengthen the wild men . . . in their cry for the extermination of the Jews.'

On 12 March 1938 the Austrian Chancellor, Kurt Schuschnigg (1897–1977), resigned. By the following evening the German annexation of Austria had been approved by the Austrian cabinet and signed by Adolf Hitler. The Führer fatefully proclaimed political union between Germany and Austria – *Anschluss* – incorporating Austria within the Third Reich and so creating a 'Greater Germany' – *Grossdeutschland*. This momentous act was greeted with joy on the streets of Vienna by thousands of people, who enthusiastically welcomed long columns of German troops and armoured vehicles. By 15 March Hitler had arrived in Vienna to address a massive, ecstatic crowd. Ominously, Heinrich Himmler and Reinhard Heydrich soon followed.

A 13-year-old Jewish boy named Lucian Meisel (or Meysels, 1925–2012) later remembered what ensued: 'As we walked back home, suddenly the mob was coming in – a howling mob, which I'd never seen before. Smashing shop windows, just

---

3 Since his death, the bishop has been the subject of controversial accusations of abuse.

barbaric. That moment we knew we had to get out, and had to get out fast.'[4] Walter Kammerling, another young Viennese Jew, agreed: 'You were completely outlawed. There was no protection from anywhere. Anybody could come up to you and do what they want . . .' A. R. Penn, Secretary of the Church's Mission to the Jews, had arrived in Vienna the day before the *Anschluss* and had meetings with Grimes. A Jewish friend took Penn to a hillside overlooking the city: 'I feel as if I am looking at my beloved Vienna for the last time,' she confided.

After the *Anschluss*, Germany's punitive Nuremberg Laws, including the *Blutschutzgesetz*, were extended to Austria, and things rapidly worsened for Vienna's Jews as Nazis called for 'the liberation of Vienna . . . from alien Jewish rule' and a 'cleansing of Jewified Austria'. Pent-up loathing and frustration boiled over into a frenzy of violence and hatred. In April, during *Pesach* (Passover), Hitler's SA (*Sturmabteilung*) set about systematically assaulting and humiliating Viennese Jews in the strongly Jewish quarter of Leopoldstadt. In Taborstrasse, SA roughs tore off the wigs worn for modesty by Orthodox Jewish women, and then taunted and mocked them as they were forced to parade in public. In the nearby Prater park, celebrated for its iconic Ferris wheel, thugs stripped and beat Jews, shaved off their beards and even made them eat human excrement. On the Reichsbrücke over the Danube, Jews were compelled to spit in one another's faces. Young Walter Kammerling was particularly shocked to see a well-dressed Viennese woman hold up her young daughter, the better to

---

4 BBC Radio 4 *Document*, 8 August 2011, presented by Mike Thomson. Meisel managed to emigrate to what was then Palestine.

watch a Nazi stormtrooper kicking an elderly Jew who had been forced to scrub the street. Stormtroopers also looted Sigmund Freud's Vienna apartment, robbing him of 6,000 Austrian schillings: 'Never have I been paid so much for a single visit,' he commented wryly.

The Vienna correspondent of the *Daily Telegraph* reported:

> Nazi storm-troopers, surrounded by jostling, jeering and laughing mobs of 'golden Viennese hearts', dragged Jews from shops, offices and homes – men and women – put scrubbing-brushes in their hands, splashed them [the brushes] well with acid, and made them go down on their knees and scrub away for hours . . . Every morning in the Habsburgergasse the S.S. squads were told how many Jews to round up for menial tasks . . . The favourite task was that of cleaning the bowls of the w.c.s in the S.S. barracks, which the Jews were forced to do simply with their naked hands.

On top of this appalling violence, a systematic 'Aryanization' (in other words, theft) of Jewish-owned businesses was set in motion, and Jewish assets and property were illegally possessed and confiscated by Austrian Nazis. Within a fortnight a systematic purge had been completed. Jews were removed from academic posts and the theatre and barred from military service. Jewish factories and department stores were seized and priceless art collections looted.

On 1 April 1938 the first of many trains left Austria, taking prisoners to Dachau concentration camp, outside Munich, Bavaria. Initially most of those transported were Hitler's political opponents, but by May the Nazis were also sending Jews they labelled 'asocial', 'criminal' or simply 'disagreeable'. Three-quarters of those transported to Dachau in 1938 were Jewish. Before ever they reached the camp, the great majority had been attacked and beaten in transit – and in some instances killed – by SS men in their death's-head uniforms. The terror that they now realized they faced resulted in many appalled Viennese Jews taking their own lives.

A Jewish family approached Grimes in April 1938 requesting proof of Christian baptism, hoping that this might enable them to emigrate to Italy. According to the writer Giles MacDonogh, Grimes began to marry Jews according to the rite of the Church of England, simultaneously conferring baptism. But this was just the beginning. It seems that Revd Grimes was also considering the possibility of offering baptism and a baptismal certificate to Jews wanting to emigrate so that their visa would describe them as Christian rather than Jewish. At *Anschluss*, the United Kingdom introduced a visa requirement for all German nationals. Possession of a baptismal certificate increased the likelihood of the British Passport Control Office, headed by Thomas Kendrick – an undercover MI6 officer – issuing a visa.

Some countries were still willing to receive baptized Jews as immigrants, and some officials were prepared to accept Jews with baptismal certificates, regardless of suspicions as to their authenticity. If they *were* able to leave, Jewish emigrants still had to pay the authorities the infamous *Fluchtsteuer* (flight tax), forfeiting most of their money and property.

Kendrick spent much effort writing to countries within the British Empire requesting the admission of Jewish refugees, but to little avail. Australia was very reluctant to admit Jews at all. At the Evian refugee conference in July 1938 the Australian representative was forthright: 'Since we don't have a real race problem, we have no wish to import one.' Likewise, in South America, Brazil refused to accept non-baptized Jews. Possession of a visa did mean, however, that Jewish fugitives en route to Palestine were able to pass through countries such as Yugoslavia and Greece, where Judaism was still classed as a religious faith and not a racial classification. In 1938 almost 3,000 Austrian Jews entered Palestine legally.

The chaplain at Christ Church could not be sure his baptism plan would succeed. Yet even if it was only minimally effective, he hoped that possession of an Anglican baptismal

The Revd Hugh Grimes   **The Revd Frederick Collard**

Courtesy Anthony Kaines, Guernsey CI

certificate might allow Jews in Vienna some form of protection, gaining them a little time to put their affairs in order before they left, or with luck helping them to obtain a transit visa for travel through neighbouring countries.

Even Jews queueing for visas became the victims of Nazi harassment, as the British Consul-General in Vienna reported:

> On Monday morning, the SA and SS brought several motor cars on to the street where the Consulate-General is situated, collected Jews from neighbouring offices and shops and forced them to wash the motor cars in pouring rain. At that time, there were great numbers of Jews in the Consulate-General applying for immigration certificates to various parts of the British empire and as they left the building they too were seized and forced to wash the cars.[5]

Kendrick told the Consul-General, Donald St Clair Gainer (1891–1966): 'My staff are so overwrought, they will burst into tears at the slightest provocation.'

Soon queues of Jews seeking baptism started to form outside Christ Church. Lori Rudov, ten years old at the time, remembered the chaplain as 'totally unruffled' when surrounded by Jewish families requesting baptism. On 14 June 1938, Revd Grimes baptized eight Jews, on 19 June 12 and on 26 June 19. On 10 July the chaplain managed to baptize as many as 103 candidates. On 23 July 1938 it became compulsory for the Austrian identity cards of all Jews to be marked with a 'J' (for *Jude*, Jew). The following day 129 Jews were baptized at the

---

5 Public Record Office FO 371/21635.

chaplaincy, reaching a peak of 229 on 25 July. At this point, Revd Grimes was recalled to London to explain his activities to the suspicious and disapproving authorities of the Church of England.[6]

The chaplain knew precisely what he was doing. He had no intention of proselytizing or converting those who came to him seeking baptism. He made no serious attempt to instruct them in Christian belief, but simply required them to recite the recently learned Catechism and the Lord's Prayer. As well as a baptismal certificate – often helpfully backdated – candidates were given a copy of the Anglican Book of Common Prayer. Women who, as children, were present at these baptisms have described the area in and around the church as 'pandemonium and chaos'.

During Grimes's absence in London, he was replaced by Revd Frederick Collard, incumbent of Cologne's Rathauskapelle (Town Hall Chapel), which he had persuaded the mayor, Konrad Adenauer (post-war Chancellor of West Germany), he could use for Anglican worship. Collard had served as a stretcher-bearer in the First World War, retiring from the army in 1924 as a major in the Royal Army Medical Corps

---

6 At the same time, Bishop Bell of Chichester and the Archbishop of York signed a letter to *The Times* on 19 July 1938: 'We have before us a credible report that since Herr Hitler and his forces entered Vienna, some 7,000 Jews have committed suicide in that city alone. The degree of suffering, terror and hopelessness thus attested defies imagination. No comment is needed on Field-Marshal Goering's wireless statement at the end of March that the Jews had better do away with themselves if they wanted to, and that he could not put a policeman behind every Jew to prevent suicides. We submit that this systematic attempt to root out and destroy the members of one of the most gifted human races in Austria and Germany has become a case of conscience for every man and woman who holds the Christian doctrine that the human personality is sacred.'

with the British Army of Occupation in Cologne.[7] In 1935 the Bishop of Fulham, Revd Basil Batty (1873–1952), ordained Collard as curate at the advanced age of 68, after which the retired major served as Batty's curate at St Anne and St Agnes Church in London before returning to Cologne. Part of Batty's duties as Bishop of Fulham was the responsibility for Anglican churches in northern and central Europe; he had told the Archbishop of Canterbury that he wanted to try to provoke German Protestants to respond to the Nazis' appalling treatment of the Jews. In the week following Grimes's departure no baptisms are recorded in the Christ Church register. However, after arriving in Vienna on 3 August, Collard immediately took up the business of baptizing where Grimes had left off.

A fortnight later matters at the British Consulate in Vienna became complicated and critical. On 16 August, Thomas Kendrick, officially Passport Control Officer but in fact MI6 Head of Vienna Station for the previous 13 years, was arrested. He had been on his way home to England via Salzburg by car with his family, possibly forewarned that trouble was brewing. Kendrick's plight became headline news: the London *News Chronicle* announced, 'Secret Police arrest British Passport Chief'. Kendrick was taken to the Hotel Metropole in Morzinplatz, commandeered by the Gestapo as their Vienna headquarters, where Schuschnigg and Louis Rothschild, head of the Austrian branch of his family, were also being held. There he was interrogated by Nazi officers for three days in eight-hour relays, before being released at noon on 20 August after having admitted he was a spy.

---

7   Kendrick was stationed in Cologne during the same period.

The previous day the Consul-General had sent a report to Sir Nevile Henderson, the British Ambassador in Berlin, following an interview with Revd Collard:

It appears that ever since March, a very large number of Jews have applied to be received into the Anglican Church. Between 13 March and 25 July, Mr Grimes has baptized some 900 Jews, including 93 on 24 July and 224 on 25 July. The applicants for baptism remain numerous and Mr Collard has been continuing the lessons and instructions in Christian tenets given by Mr Grimes and has himself received a very large number of Jews into the church. As the work was very heavy, Mr Collard looked around for clerical assistance and a baptized Jew named [Edmund] Pollitzer presented himself with a recommendation from Mr Grimes and was employed in making out baptismal certificates for Mr Collard's signature. From time to time, Mr Pollitzer gave Mr Collard sums of money for the Church contributed by the Jewish converts. On Tuesday 16 August, the same day upon which the Gestapo called to arrest Captain Kendrick, the Police raided the flat, where a number of Jews were congregated, searched the place, confiscated the registers and declared the baptismal certificates had been issued pre-dated and that Pollitzer had been receiving RM. [*Reichsmarks*] 50 each for these false certificates.

It has been suggested the Gestapo were linking Revds Grimes and Collard to a spy ring centred on Thomas Kendrick. Kendrick was a major player in the SIS in the 1930s and had been running an important British espionage operation attempting to obtain information about German shipyards and submarines, in particular such new battleships as the *Tirpitz* being constructed at Wilhelmshaven naval base.

The German authorities now ordered Kendrick to leave the German Reich within 24 hours and the entire MI6 operation in Vienna was closed down. At the same time Frank Foley, head of the MI6 Station in Berlin, was recalled with his staff. As Passport Control Officer in Berlin, Foley had facilitated the escape of thousands of Jews and is recognized as one of the Righteous Among the Nations.[8] The disaster in Vienna has been described as the worst British intelligence blunder until the notorious incident at Venlo during the phoney war.[9] Following his expulsion, Kendrick landed at Croydon Airport on Monday 22 August, a photograph of him appearing in the next morning's *Daily Telegraph*. Eric Gedye, reporter for the *Morning Chronicle*, also suspected of spying, was ordered to leave Vienna at the same time.

Fred 'Siegfried' Richter was arrested two days after Kendrick, on 14 August. Richter was a Jewish-born former racehorse trainer who worked as a clerk at the British Consulate and also served as verger at the Anglican chaplaincy. Richter was married to an Irishwoman, had taken British nationality and had joined the Anglican Church. When he was arrested, the

8   The story of Frank Foley is told in Michael Smith, *Foley: The spy who saved 10,000 Jews*, Hodder & Stoughton, London, 1999.

9   For an account of the Venlo incident, see Max Hastings, *The Secret War: Spies, codes and guerrillas 1939–45*, William Collins, London, 2015, pp. 44–7.

Gestapo found 2,000 Reichsmarks on him, which they used as a pretext for charging him with currency offences. He had apparently been receiving fees for locating potential agents for Kendrick's spying activities and was also being recompensed as verger of Christ Church for introducing Jews to Grimes as candidates for baptism. Kendrick was possibly betrayed by a German double agent named Karl Tucek, who had been meeting Richter – and Kendrick at least once – in the chaplaincy. On Tucek's evidence, Richter was sentenced to 12 years' imprisonment and died at Auschwitz.[10]

Meanwhile, on 20 August Adolf Eichmann, determined to force Jews out of German territories (preferably bound for Palestine), set up the Central Agency for Jewish Emigration at the expropriated Rothschild Palace in Vienna. Hearing something of the horrors of Dachau, experiencing the insults and abuse of officials and being conscious of the continuing terror on the city's streets, thousands of Jews queued at his agency to obtain exit visas. By the end of 1938, Eichmann had succeeded in expelling 80,000 Austrian Jews, having first fleeced them with the *Fluchtsteuer*.

On the day of Kendrick's release, the Gestapo raided the chaplain's apartment at Lustig-Prean-Gasse 10,[11] where they found Fred Collard instructing 32 Jews in the Anglican faith. The Nazi operatives dispersed the Jews and detained Revd Collard along with an unnamed woman and the previously mentioned Edmund Henry Pollitzer, a Viennese Jew and

---

10 Tucek had been a member of the Nazi Party in Austria at a time when it was proscribed and was a friend of Ernst Kaltenbrunner (1903–46), later *Obergruppenführer* in the SS.

11 The fascists' new name for Jaurèsgasse.

**Adolf Eichmann at his 1961 war crimes trial in Israel.
He was executed in 1962**
Wiki commons: Israel Government Press Office

former lecturer and journalist who had been baptized on
12 July. Unlike Hugh Grimes, Collard did not enjoy diplomatic
immunity, so he was hauled off by the Gestapo to the Hotel
Metropole. There the elderly cleric was interrogated and badly
shaken up. Eventually released, but fearing for his safety,

Collard requested a police escort before he returned to Grimes's flat, to find that it had been ransacked and the church's baptismal register confiscated by the Gestapo.

Despite this setback, Revd Collard continued heroically baptizing Jews. The Gestapo returned his register, presumably after having noted the names inscribed in it, and queues soon reappeared outside the chaplaincy. Collard now started performing baptisms on alternate days, giving him sufficient time to hear candidates rehearse the Catechism and the Lord's Prayer before proceeding. Like Grimes, Collard baptized candidates of all ages, from babes in arms to 80-year-olds, and by mid-September, when he was removed by the Anglican establishment, he had baptized a total of 800 Jews.

An unexpected source of evidence of these events is George Lane-Fox Pitt-Rivers (1890–1966), a member of Mosley's British Union of Fascists, a eugenicist and anti-Semite, and one of the wealthiest Englishmen of the interwar years.[12] Pitt-Rivers witnessed the activities of Collard in Vienna, and, with his own caustic slant, afforded more light on what was happening. He reported that Christ Church was temporarily closed in the summer of 1938 for cleaning and redecoration, so the 'good work of "conversion" was proceeding with the utmost possible despatch', with baptisms carried out at an 'improvised font' in the 'office chapel' – Hugh Grimes's flat – opposite the church in Lustig-Prean-Gasse. Pitt-Rivers pointed out that few of the candidates could speak English, instruction in the 'tenets of

---

12 During the Second World War, Pitt-Rivers was interned as a Nazi sympathizer at Brixton Prison and Ascot internment centre.

the faith and in the Catechism' lasted less than four hours, and that the interval between application for baptism and its enactment was less than four days – 'not too long a period for those who cannot speak a word of English'. He finished with a sarcastic rhetorical flourish:

> it is through the Anglican door of baptismal waters that alien Jews can most rapidly prepare for 'assimilation and absorption' in their new English homeland, flowing with milk – canned in Switzerland [possibly a reference to the League of Nations] and imported under arrangements of the Milk Marketing Board, and honey – imported from [Communist] Russia under arrangements of the Board of Trade.

The majority of the applicants for baptism were Viennese, since most Austrian Jews lived in the capital. Some originated in the Burgenland, on the eastern border of Austria, but had been driven out by Aryanizing purges. A number planned to try to emigrate to Australia and hoped Anglican baptism might ease their course. By September an increasing number of Hungarian Jews were also seeking baptism, possibly because by this date Hungarians were only being readmitted to their native country if they could prove they were Christian. As mentioned later, these baptisms provoked a protest from a Church of Scotland minister in Budapest.

On 15 September Bishop Batty sent Fred Collard back to his church in Cologne, an act that coincided with Neville Chamberlain's Munich appeasement mission. The following month Batty went to Vienna to appoint the Revd F. A. Evelyn, 'an experienced priest', as a permanent replacement for Hugh Grimes. There had been discussion about sending Grimes back to Vienna, but it was feared he would be arrested by the Gestapo. The British Foreign Secretary, Lord Halifax, wrote to the Archbishop of Canterbury informing him that 'it has not been possible to proceed with the appointment of Revd Grimes'. The new chaplain, Revd Evelyn, was instructed to be much more circumspect in his practice of baptism.

The entries in the Christ Church registers, which are preserved at the church, allow some analysis of the candidates for what Giles MacDonogh has dubbed 'political baptism'. Since it was the Church of England offering baptism, the intended destination of many of the applicants was probably the United Kingdom, its colonies and dominions, as well as the USA. Pitt-Rivers reported that the baptismal certificates were issued 'in order to qualify in England under the schemes of the "Churches' Committee for Non-Aryan Christians" and other associated bodies'. This committee had been formed by Bishop George Bell in 1937 to raise money to support 'new Christians' arriving in Britain. Pitt-Rivers added that those requesting baptism had to be in possession of: 'a) a British visa, b) an *Ausweis* or release from the *Jüdischer Kultur Bund* [sic] or Jewish congregation; and c) the German police permit to leave the country – and not return.'

Many newly baptized Jews escaped Austria via Yugoslavia, where as yet no anti-Semitic laws had been passed. As long as an individual possessed a certificate describing him or her as Christian rather than Jewish, he or she would be able to enter a country where Judaism was still regarded as a religious – rather than racial – matter and hence not a bar.

Otto Bovensiepen (1905–79),[13] SS *Untersturmführer* in Eisenstadt, Austria, was well aware of what was going on in Vienna, reporting on 11 August 1938: 'A number of Jews have taken the decision to have themselves baptized according to the Anglican rite in order to obtain permission to cross Yugoslavia and enter Greece.'

By the time Grimes's and Collard's exceptional baptisms were stopped, as many as 1,800 Jews had been given baptismal certificates, of whom it has been claimed that all but 100 survived the war. Of that minority, most were arrested elsewhere in Europe.

Those baptized by Grimes and Collard include a number of well-known names. The composer Arthur Kleiner (1903–80) escaped finally to the USA, where he was responsible for the music added to silent films such as *Battleship Potemkin* (1925) and *Metropolis* (1927). Erich Zeisl (1905–59), who later wrote music for the film *The Postman Always Rings Twice* (1946), left Vienna after the *Kristallnacht* violence of 9 November 1938, narrowly escaping arrest in Cologne before travelling to Paris and to the USA in September 1939. His wife had discovered a completely unrelated Arnold Zeissl [sic] in Milwaukee who agreed to provide necessary documentation. Erich's brother Egon Zeisl also escaped to the USA: his great-nephew Randolph ('Randy') Schoenberg still has the baptism certificate issued at Christ Church in 1938 and remembers the work of the Revd Grimes gratefully:

---

13 Bovensiepen later became Head of the SS in Denmark, and in September 1948 was sentenced to death for his war crimes. In 1950 this was commuted to a life sentence, yet in 1953 he was released and became managing director of a German insurance company in Mülheim an der Ruhr.

I think what Grimes did was an act of bravery and defiance . . . He had been ordered not to do these things, yet he saw desperate people in need and offered them at least a hope of escape from Austria. I think he really is an unsung hero of that terrible period.

The Zeisl brothers' father and stepmother both died at the Treblinka death camp in Poland.

Another survivor baptized at Christ Church was Dr Stefan Popper (d. 2016), who in England later presided over the discredited first inquest into the Hillsborough disaster of 1989. As a six-year-old he was baptized at Christ Church, along with his twin sister. Later, living safely in Britain as a 12-year-old, he told his father he wanted to convert from Judaism to Christianity, only to discover he had already been baptized in Vienna! Others who obtained baptismal certificates included the eminent Viennese architects Oskar Neumann (1870–1951), famous for his distinctive Art Nouveau decorative style, and Oskar Wlach (1881–1963), who designed residential buildings in Vienna but died destitute in New York after emigrating. Margaret Bettelheim, sister of the well-known child psychiatrist and author Bruno Bettelheim (1903–90), was also baptized in Vienna.

On 25 August 1938 Hugh Grimes was interviewed in London for the Foreign Office by Gladwyn, later Lord, Jebb (1900–96). Although the Consul-General in Vienna suspected Grimes of being involved along with Kendrick in espionage, the Foreign Office did not believe he had any links with MI6. Grimes was eager to return to Vienna – he even offered to forgo his £300 annual stipend – but was successfully dissuaded.

Despite the chaplains' success in allowing unknown numbers of Jews to leave Austria, there were strong misgivings within the Anglican establishment. In December 1938 Archbishop Cosmo Lang's secretary wrote to Basil Batty questioning the authenticity of the Vienna baptisms, following a complaint from the Church of Scotland chaplain in Budapest, Revd George A. Knight, that 'the chaplain [in Vienna] has accepted Jews and baptized them, without any preparation whatsoever . . . in batches of fifty a day . . . this practice, if continued, is likely to cause a good deal of scandal',[14] adding that Grimes's activities in Vienna were causing problems in Hungary.

The Bishop of Fulham strongly defended Grimes's actions. He started by pointing out, perhaps disingenuously: 'We have our mission to the Jews and it is difficult for a priest to refuse to deal with a Jew who wishes to become a Christian . . .' He went on to claim that Grimes was 'a scholar and a gentleman in whom I have confidence. I think it must be admitted that his [Grimes's] intense sympathy with these poor people in their terrible suffering led him to a greater belief in their sincerity than an outsider would have done.' He further defended Grimes by saying, 'It is a fact that a number of Jews were baptized, but the statement that they were baptized without any preparation is *absolutely untrue* [his emphasis]. The preparation given was carefully thought out and I was assured that it covered all that was essential.'

Evidently, Grimes's permanent replacement, Revd F. A. Evelyn, continued to offer baptism to significant numbers of Jews wishing to emigrate, but with much greater scrutiny. Batty claimed, 'He has been instructed that the greatest care must be

---

14 George Knight's work in Budapest is described in Chapter 3, about Jane Haining.

taken in these cases and long [baptismal] preparation given. Also that if there is the slightest ground for believing that baptism is wanted on political grounds, it must be refused.'

The complaints continued. Mrs Elsie Ludovici, of Upper Norwood, London, wrote to Archbishop Lang on 12 January 1939, 'horrified to hear that mass baptisms had been taking place in Vienna, that [Jews] were being admitted at the rate of as many as 900 [!] a day into the Anglican Church . . . merely for the purpose of benefiting from the charities organized for the help of Christians.' The archbishop was assured by his chaplain and secretary Alan Don (1885–1966) that her accusations – apparently originating from Pitt-Rivers – were 'grotesquely untrue'.

The Anglican authorities were naturally concerned that what they regarded as one of their church's solemn sacraments might be being abused, employed as a pragmatic device to allow Jews to obtain documents declaring them Christian. Even such a sympathetic figure as Bishop George Bell of Chichester, an early and outspoken opponent of Hitler's anti-Semitic campaigns, wrote to Alan Don 'very much perturbed . . . about the baptism of Jews in Vienna'.

There has also been debate about the practical efficacy of baptism certificates. David Cesarani pointed out that 'the certificate was by no stretch of the imagination a travel document . . . Besides, Jews had a large "J" (for *Jude*) stamped in their passports'. Yet Giles MacDonogh notes that this practice had not come into effect by September 1938, when his own Jewish grandfather left Austria without such a stamp.

In any event, Thomas Kendrick helped around 200 Jews a day to escape Austria in the summer of 1938, something which has been overlooked until recently, probably because of the uproar concerning his arrest and expulsion. Among others who succeeded in emigrating were the eminent dermatologist Dr Erwin Pulay (1889–1950), grandfather of the British actor Roger Lloyd-Pack; the conductor Erwin Stein (1885–1958), whose daughter was to marry first the seventh Earl of Harewood and later the disgraced Liberal politician Jeremy Thorpe; and 19-year-old George Weidenfeld (1919–2016), who later co-founded the British publishing house Weidenfeld and Nicolson.

Both Grimes and Collard continued their clerical callings. Just before the Second World War, the Revd Grimes managed to fit in a visit to Palestine, presumably confirming his concern for the Jews. After this he held further chaplaincy posts briefly, first in Dinant, then in Biarritz, where he was regarded as an *espion actif* (active spy) and apparently escaped by walking over the Pyrenees into neutral Spain. In 1942 Hugh Grimes was appointed rector of Newton Ferrers, Devon, where he also achieved a certain local notoriety for skinny-dipping. By 1945 he had familiarized himself sufficiently with the village to write a chatty visitors' guide, the *History of Newton Ferrers*, which sold for one shilling and sixpence. The booklet concludes with his college motto *Prosperum iter facias* – 'May your journey be successful.' Is it far-fetched to see this as a coded message?

From 1939 till 1942, and then again after 1945, Revd Frederick Collard was curate of St Michel du Valle, Vale, on the German-occupied Channel Island of Guernsey. For the last three years of the war he acted as curate at St Stephen's Church, Guernsey, after the vicar, Revd T. Hartley Jackson, and assistant priest, Revd S. W. Gerhold, were both deported to a Nazi internment camp.[15] Despite his encounter with the Gestapo in Vienna, he survived on Guernsey and died in 1959, at the age of 90. He is said never to have spoken of his Viennese past.

A memorial plaque, with an image of the baptismal registers, to commemorate the achievements of Grimes and Collard was unveiled at Christ Church, Vienna, at evensong on 18 May 2013. Dr Harold Chipman, whose grandfather was among those baptized in 1938, spoke at the service.

---

15 Revd Jackson had sent a Christmas message to *The Star*, the local paper, which the German press officer changed to read: 'The recognition that Christ was born into the world to save the world and bring peace on earth is the need of Britain and her Jewish and Bolshevik allies.' The vicar protested strongly from his pulpit on Christmas morning. Nine months later, when the Nazis deported for internment in Germany those who were not permanent Guernsey residents, Jackson was included among them, despite the Dean of Guernsey pleading for his exemption as an invalid. Ralph Durand, *Guernsey under German Rule*: Guernsey Society, Guernsey, 2018.

3

The borders of heaven

JANE HAINING, BUDAPEST

Jane Haining was born a Scottish farmer's daughter at the end of the nineteenth century; she died almost certainly in the gas chambers of Auschwitz-Birkenau 47 years later after she refused to desert the Jewish children under her care in Nazi-occupied Budapest.

Born on 6 June 1897 at Lochenhead, Dumfries, in south-west Scotland, Jane was the fifth child in her family. Her mother died when she was only five, after which a relative cared for the children while their father, Thomas Haining, worked his farm. Her biographer sketched Jane's character thus: 'Jovial she seldom was, though of happy disposition; there was a root in her of gravity . . . which went well with the characteristic dry humour of the countryside.'[1]

Jane did well at school and in 1909 won a scholarship to Dumfries Academy, alma mater of several distinguished Scots, including Revd Dr Henry Duncan (1774–1846), founder of the

---

1   David McDougall, ed. Ian Alexander, *Jane Haining of Budapest*, The Church of Scotland World Mission, Edinburgh, 1998.

world's first commercial savings bank, J. M. Barrie, author of *Peter Pan*, and John Laurie, celebrated for his role as Private Frazer in *Dad's Army*. Jane was one of the first boarders at the school's Moat Hostel and graduated as 'dux', or top pupil. She then trained at the Commercial College of Glasgow Athenaeum, before working as a secretary for ten years at the celebrated Paisley threadmaker J. & P. Coats Ltd.

A churchgoer and Sunday School teacher, Jane began to take an interest in Christian missions. After attending a meeting of the Church of Scotland Jewish Mission Committee, where Revd Dr George Mackenzie spoke of his activities in eastern and central Europe, she told a friend, 'I have found my life's work'. Jane now started to prepare for her new vocation, leaving her job and earning a diploma and certificate in housekeeping at the Glasgow School of Domestic Science, while also learning German at evening classes. Jane next responded to an opening advertised in *Life and Work*, the magazine of the Church of Scotland, for a matron/superintendent at the girls' hostel of the Scottish Jewish Committee Mission School in Budapest. Selected for the post, Jane left Scotland on 20 June 1932, following her thirty-fifth birthday and after further training at St Colm's Women's Missionary College in Edinburgh. A letter sent to a cousin shortly after Jane's appointment reveals her own shock at the move: 'I am afraid it was almost as big a surprise to me as anyone to find myself appointed to a Missionary post but I am very happy in my work . . . I found myself appointed almost before I could believe it myself, so you see I approached not from the Missionary side but from the Girls' Home side.'

The Budapest mission was originally set up by John 'Rabbi' Duncan in August 1841 with the aim of converting Jewish

**The impressive Scottish Mission premises at Vörösmarty
utca 51, Budapest, where Jane Haining served as matron to
schoolgirl boarders**
Wiki commons odd wellies

people to Christianity, although under Hungarian law only
those aged 18 and over could convert. The impressive mission premises at 51 Vörösmarty Street comprised a five-storey
building around a central courtyard, with classrooms and living quarters interlinked by open terraces. The school aimed to
offer a good education; roughly three-quarters of its pupils were

Jewish, many of them orphans or from poor families. Only a minority of the pupils boarded in the fourth-floor girls' hostel, consisting of two bedrooms with about 16 girls in each room.

Soon after she arrived, Jane described her work:

> There are about 400 pupils ranging in age from six to sixteen, and of these about thirty to forty either live in or are day-boarders in the Institute for which I am responsible. We try to surround these girls with a Christian home atmosphere and, without trying to thrust religion down their throats, to instil into them, consciously or subconsciously, by practice as well as precept, what Christianity means.

Yet from the age of ten the girls had a very intensive religious education, as described by a former pupil, Judith Szabó:

> Every day would start with Bible classes. We had proper Protestant education . . . We had Bible reading during breakfast, and we had to pray in the morning, at lunchtime and in the evening. Miss Haining was very religious and this was how she brought us up. There was Sunday school every Sunday morning, and then service, for four years. But there was also Jewish religious education, and they took us to the Synagogue . . . quite often on Jewish holidays [presumably at least five times a year].

Since the law did not permit religious conversion for under-18s, the school aimed to prepare its Jewish students for later conversion to Christianity.

Jane Haining with some of the girls from the Budapest hostel at Lake Balaton, Hungary in the 1930s

Church of Scotland

Jane arrived during the summer holidays and took a small group of boarders to stay beside Lake Balaton, the nearest thing Hungary had to a seaside resort. Once term began, she got down to work as matron. Although she had enough German to communicate with her pupils, she now started to learn the difficult Hungarian language. Jane eventually became quite proficient, though her Hungarian was always spoken with a distinct Scots accent.

Jane soon connected with her pupils. Years later, a pupil named Ibolya Surányi remembered her impressions of both matron and mission:

I started school in 1935 at the age of six. Our home was on the third floor . . . our favourite place was a big open terrace. That was the room where we played together – forty to fifty children – and Jane Haining was always with us. She was my second mother, who had a very important influence on my life. She was a remarkable woman. She was a mother for all of us and she treated us all equally. She was strict on certain things but she was lovely. She had a fantastic heart; you always felt that you were the one she loved the most. She gave herself fully to us. Every second Sunday afternoon we were allowed a visit by our parents. If nobody came for a child, she invited the sad kid, and at the end of the conversation the sad girl became a happy girl.

Other students reported a similar combination of strictness and security. One remembered: 'Our beloved Miss Haining made us grow used to order and discipline.' And another:

'I felt like a martyr as we had to wear black stockings and the drills seemed like being in a prison. But as an adult I am grateful for the Spartan way of life as that has helped me through a lot of hardships.' A third pupil, Katalin Packard, recalled strict rules about hair: 'I went to my father's family for the summer and they put a permanent wave in my hair, and I felt so beautiful. I went back to school with the curly hair. Well I was not allowed. She put me in pigtails.'

Jane wrote home in 1937:

We have one new little six-year-old going to school for the first time, but an orphan without either father or mother. She is such a pathetic wee soul to look at and I fear, poor lamb, has been in not too good surroundings before she came to us . . . She certainly does look as though she needs heaps and heaps of love. One other is such a nice child. Her father is dead and the mother left for America in June to try and make a home and a living for them both there, and yet one never hears a complaint from her of loneliness, which is so different to another who still cries herself to sleep every night.

A letter home to Dr George Mackenzie, whose lecture had first interested Jane in the mission, seems to indicate that she felt that intensive Christian indoctrination had its limitations: 'if a child has a daily Bible lesson, besides a religion lesson twice a week . . . goes to Sunday School and Church every Sunday and has the Bible read to her twice daily, well it would not be any great wonder if she was just a little stawed [overfull] would it?' Her preferred method seems to have been 'trying to surround [a child] with the atmosphere of a Christian home and . . . keep on trying to teach her what are the implications of Christian love in the incidents of everyday life'.

As early as the winter of 1938 the school took in four refugee children from Austria, where violent oppression of the Jews followed the *Anschluss* in March.[2] In Hungary, too, hatred of the Jews was becoming much more overt. Jane wrote, 'What a ghastly feeling it must be to know that no one wants you and to feel that your neighbours literally grudge you your daily bread.' Unrest in Budapest began to affect the children, some of whose behaviour became more difficult as a result.

In the early 1930s Hungary had passed anti-Semitic legislation. Then in February 1938 the 'first Jewish law' was passed, defining Jews by a mixture of descent and race. A more draconian second Jewish law was passed in November 1938, by which Jews were recognized solely on a racial basis, lost their political rights and were barred from employment in the arts and journalism or by the state. Jane wrote to a friend about a Jewish girl at the mission who longed to become a teacher but under Hungarian law would no longer be allowed to do so. She also wrote of a Jewish mother of twins who 'was thinking of adding some poison to their food and ending it all'.

In April 1935, the Revd George A. F. Knight had been appointed to take charge of the mission in Budapest. He avowed strong opposition to the mounting anti-Semitism in Europe and claimed to be 'repelled by the idea of proselytism', yet commended the mission's evangelistic methods for its Jewish pupils: 'One of the most effective methods of

---

2   As described in Chapter 2.

training the girls to be true Christian women is to have them constantly under one's care in the atmosphere of a Christian home.' While boldly attacking the Hungarian fascist Arrow Cross movement, Knight's report to his mission HQ in Edinburgh invidiously distinguished between Budapest's 'true Hungarians' and Jews.

Knight also acted as unofficial chaplain to the British Legation. In his memoirs, published more than 30 years after the war, he wrote:

> Many of the British community were young girls who greatly needed a pastor. The British Consul and I each kept a list of these girls. A man would phone up and say 'Can you provide a girl to give me English conversation lessons?' Usually he added, 'She must be young and pretty.' After following up such girls to hospital perhaps suffering from syphilis, I would earnestly urge them to get back home to England.[3]

It is difficult to understand why he believed that what appears to have amounted to procuring was part of his role.

In late 1938 officials of Arrow Cross raided the mission, accusing Knight and his colleagues of contravening Hungarian law by helping refugees. This resulted in a strong statement to her staff by the Hungarian headmistress, Edit Roda, on 7 December: 'It is not a secret that this institute is a Jewish Mission, and that most of our pupils are Jewish. The

---

3   George A. F. Knight, *What Next?*, Saint Andrew Press, Edinburgh, 1980, p. 34.

management reminds everyone that anyone who sympathises with xenophobic views cannot work here.'

Around this time, with oppression growing steadily stronger, the mission started to stage Wednesday-evening concerts, with audiences of up to four hundred, when persecuted Jewish artists and musicians performed, in an effort to provide them with paid work and to lift morale.

George Knight also trod a perilous path politically. Two secret service operatives from the British Legation persuaded him to liaise with pro-Western members of the Hungarian government and to supply radios for Jewish observers he recruited to report on German shipping movements on the Danube. 'I undertook to go by car after dark to places 100–150 miles up the Danube with radio transmitters hidden in the boot,' he recorded. 'But beforehand I went scouting to find the right persons . . . to undertake a watch on the Danube for unusual barge movements and then be willing and able to transmit a signal to the Legation in Budapest. The people I selected were always Jews . . . I was able to fit up those transmitters in people's homes and teach them how to operate them . . . In the end . . . the Nazis did not enter Hungary down the Danube but, in 1944, across the plains in their tanks.'[4]

Jane returned home to Scotland for a break in the summer of 1939, accompanied by Margit Prém, the Hungarian headmistress of the mission's elementary school and a 'born speechifier', with whom Jane seems to have developed a particularly close friendship, which apparently provoked the jealousy of at least one Hungarian friend. The two women

---

4   Knight, *What Next?*, p. 51.

spoke at public meetings, describing their work and the oppression of Jews that they had witnessed in Hungary. In September, while holidaying in Cornwall, they heard that Britain had declared war on Germany. Although Jane's friends and family were naturally concerned for her safety, she determined to return to Budapest. 'The journey back was a nightmare,' she wrote home; 'five changes, no porters, no hot food, crowded trains like Bank Holiday, plus luggage, no sanitary conveniences fit to mention, two nights spent on the platform beside, or on, our luggage.'

Further confusion awaited them at the mission in Budapest. Some staff wanted to leave immediately. It may have been at this time that young Magda Birraux overheard a heated conversation between Jane Haining and George Knight, the head of the mission, who took his family back to Scotland in time to address his church's General Assembly in 1940. 'We had a minister called Mr Knight and he lived in the house with his wife and child before the war broke out,' remembered Magda. Her story continued:

> He told Miss Haining that he was joining the Army as a chaplain and asked her to give up her job, leave everything to the school governess, and return to Scotland with him. We overheard that because our dormitory was beside Miss Haining's office and rooms. He talked very loudly and was angry that Miss Haining appeared not to understand that soon the war would break out [between Britain and Hungary]. He told her, 'You are in danger, you are an alien.' But she said, 'I have to stay here because the governess would not be able to manage.'

Yet Jane wrote home reassuringly:

I am glad to say we are shaking down into something
like order, although it was a month after I came back
before I was able to have one complete afternoon off
duty . . . The children are gradually getting into harness
and I am having time to miss the letters which do not
come.

She added circumspectly:

Of the war, it is better not to speak and indeed there is
nothing to say in a letter. Hungary is neutral and anxious
to remain so, so we, who are enjoying her hospitality, are
refraining from talking politics.

In 1940, after the Wehrmacht had overrun France and
the Netherlands in rapid blitzkrieg operations, the mission
instructed all its staff to return home while still able. Jane
wrote to the mission committee in May confirming that she
intended to stay on, claiming she faced no significant risk
and needed to stay with her children. She took responsibility for her decision and told Frances Lee, another expatriate in Budapest, 'I am the only English-speaking person left
on the staff of the Mission. The Jews are now entering their
most dangerous period – nothing would induce me to desert
them.' When the mission sent her an urgent cable pleading
with her to leave, if necessary via Istanbul and Palestine, Jane
responded with her own telegram: 'Unable travel alone stop
No British leaving stop Local conditions favour remaining –

Jane Haining.' The mission committee's response was to inform her that she remained at her own risk.

Jane wrote to her sister Nan: 'If these children need me in the days of sunshine, how much more do they need me in the days of darkness.' Her sister said later: 'She would never have had a moment's happiness if she had come home and left the children.' After this, communication with Scotland became sporadic.

In Hungary's final election before the outbreak of war, the extreme right-wing Arrow Cross Party had won 30 per cent of the vote and pushed for the segregation of the Jews. Hungary was already behaving as an ally of Germany, and in December 1941 Britain declared war against her. This hugely increased the peril for Jane Haining – as did the hope vested in the mission school by Jewish families that the Church of Scotland might offer their children sanctuary. A Budapest Jew said that the mission was regarded as a refuge from rape and deportation for Jewish girls: 'Jewish parents put their girls there for an English education. As things got worse, they put them in there hoping that, being under the protection of the Scottish mission, they would escape.' Further anti-Semitic laws were passed in 1941, prohibiting marriage between Christians and Jews, while yet more oppressive legislation the following year allowed the expropriation of Jewish-controlled rural estates.

After the outbreak of war, and particularly after 1941, Jewish refugees from elsewhere in German-occupied Europe began to arrive in Hungary. Despite the country's overt anti-Semitism, it remained relatively safe for Jews compared with neighbouring countries. Haining herself seems to have regarded the mission home as a sanctuary for Jewish refugees. After her death, a Church of Scotland leader reported, 'Mission staff spent a hectic time attempting to aid . . . émigrés to continue their flight to Great Britain and the Western hemisphere. We established a training school for prospective domestic servants and Miss Haining . . . gave courses of lectures to Jewish refugees on British conditions.'

By this date, the mission school had 315 pupils, 224 of them Jewish; of these pupils 48 were boarders, 31 of them Jewish. Jane was now kept extremely busy sourcing food for her children. On market days she got up at 5 a.m. to visit the markets to obtain provisions for the home, carrying back heavy bags of food. She is even said to have cut up her leather luggage to repair girls' shoes.

With travel to Scotland now virtually impossible, the mission was put under the emergency supervision of the Hungarian Reformed Church – which had a similar theology to that of the Church of Scotland – to ensure its work continued and its staff were paid. A new Mission Council was set up, chaired by Margit Prém, with a Hungarian minister, Revd Dr Louis Nagybaczoni Nagy, and Jane Haining as its other members. In 1942 Nagy suspended the mission's six-week class on 'the beliefs and tenets of the Reformed faith', which had previously been required before baptism. He defended his action thus:

I felt that this had become necessary because . . . restrictive civil laws concerning the Jews were being enacted and dangerous, life-threatening events were casting their shadows. Those who came to us during and after 1942 saw a life-saving potency in the piece of paper which certified that they were baptised . . . those persons were not making the conversion out of their free will and choice, circumstances forced them to do it . . . it would not [have been] humane to burden them further with another act of force, and therefore I suspended the six-week introductory course.

The mission not only set aside its previous attempts to convert the Jewish pupils, but now also provided on request a baptismal certificate for any newly arrived Jewish children, in the hope that this might help protect them. Although in 1938 George Knight had complained to the Anglican authorities about such a policy being implemented by the Revd Hugh Grimes in Vienna, the Revd Nagy now justified doing so, given the dangerous situation currently prevailing in Budapest.

During this period, Louis Nagy and Jane Haining made visits to British prisoners of war held in camps in southern Hungary, taking them books, medicine and money. Although they had the permission of the Hungarian War Office to visit, they were contravening regulations by distributing gifts – and particularly in one instance by donating a wireless. 'I shall never forget the faces of the boys,' Jane wrote, 'when we tuned in to London on Christmas Day 1943.'

The mission's teachers clearly did all they could to protect the children from the terrors outside the school. Susannah Koranyi, née Spiegel, who attended the school between 1939 and 1944, later recollected, 'As long as possible, until March 19, 1944, the day of the German occupation, everything, all the dreadful events, were kept outside the mission walls. We were children, equals – Jewish and Christian – and nothing except knowledge counted.'

In March 1944 the situation worsened drastically. The German Wehrmacht invaded Hungary, and on 21 March SS-*Obersturmbannführer* Adolf Eichmann arrived in Budapest with his *Sondereinsatzkommando Ungarn* ('special intervention unit Hungary') to take charge of Jewish deportations, knowing that he could rely on the strong support of the Hungarian authorities. On 31 March a new batch of severe anti-Jewish restrictions was introduced: Jews were forbidden to own cars or radios, use telephones, move home, wear school uniform or use public baths, swimming pools, public restaurants, cafés or bars. Jewish lawyers, civil servants and journalists were dismissed, Gentiles were forbidden to work in Jewish households and books written by Jews were banned from publication. Every Jew aged six or over had to wear a 10 x 10 cm yellow Star of David on the chest of their outer clothing. Years later Katalin Packard, one of Jane's pupils, remembered, 'On the streets there were these very big posters, and they were showing Jewish people in a very terrible picture. With horns and with a big nose and with an ugly mouth . . . Everywhere on the buildings there were these horrible pictures. That's what affected me terribly.'

In mid-April 1944 the SS started to move Jews into restricted holding areas in Budapest, including cramped ghettos and brick factories, where they were detained for weeks with little to eat. As soon as mid-July 437,403 Jews had been deported from internment camps in Hungary to Auschwitz.

The Jewish children at the mission were now required to wear the Star of David. Former pupils said Jane Haining cried as she sewed on these badges, though she told the girls they needn't wear them in the hostel. She allowed no newspapers into the boarding house, to prevent her charges from reading about the horrors of the war. The anxiety and privations were taking a physical toll on Jane: she lost weight, her hair turned white and in the summer of 1942 she had to undergo an operation for gallstones.

Soon after the invasion, and in response to the new law banning non-Jews from working in Jewish homes, Haining had dismissed the mission home's Hungarian cook, Mrs Kovacs, whose daughter Vanda was married to a man named Schréder, a member of the Hungarian fascist Arrow Cross Party. When Haining discovered that Schréder had moved into the cook's room and was eating some of the home's scarce food, she confronted him angrily. He left, threatening reprisals. Andrew Jamieson from the British Legation alleged that Schréder subsequently denounced Jane Haining to the Nazis.

According to a letter written around 1946 by Bishop László Ravasz of the Hungarian Church, between 4 and 7 April 1944 two Gestapo operatives came to the mission and searched Jane's office and bedroom. They then arrested her and gave her 15 minutes to prepare to leave. Although Jane possessed a safe-conduct document from the Swiss Legation, this was ignored, and her Bible was tossed on the floor. She left calmly. A Hungarian teacher named Otti Töth watched her being marched out of the building: 'She was wearing a smart suit. As she passed she looked up, waved and called out, "I'll be back soon!"'

She never returned.

A pupil who also saw her leave wrote later, 'The days of horror were coming, and Miss Haining protested against

Jane Haining
Church of Scotland

those who wanted to distinguish between the child of one race and the child of another. A long time later, I realized that she had died for me and the others.' One report claims that within an hour of Jane's arrest, her pupils were dispersed, hidden and given new names, as staff feared for their safety.

A colleague's diary recorded that on 30 April Jane was taken to 'the cellars of Police HQ' – possibly the Svábhegy prison, the Hotel Lomic or the Gestapo headquarters – and that 'a charwoman denounced her for having a secret radio receiver'. Jane seems next to have been taken for interrogation to a 'Gestapo villa' on the Buda hills, confiscated from a wealthy Jewish family, and then to the Hotel Belvedere. She was then transferred to the Fö utca Prison in central Budapest. Friends and colleagues tried to discover what had happened and eventually found out where she was being held. They took her food parcels and changes of underwear.

Frances Lee, a fellow expatriate and prisoner at Fö utca, said later:

> I remember very clearly the day she brought this list [of charges] from the Svábhegy prison where she had been 'questioned'. She read them out laughingly to me saying she had felt such a 'stupid' repeating *Ja, es ist wahr* ['Yes, that is true'] after each accusation, except the sixth (that she had been involved in politics). She said she had been too busy to occupy herself with politics.

Lee also reported that Haining was interrogated twice and emerged claiming the charges were 'ridiculous', optimistic that she would shortly be released.

Frances Lee recorded the long list of charges against Haining: working with Jewish girls; crying when she saw the yellow Star of David with the word *Jude* on her girls' uniforms, realizing this would mark them out for persecution and possible deportation; dismissing the hostel's Aryan cook; listening to the BBC news on the radio; receiving many British guests; visiting British prisoners of war and sending them relief parcels; and engaging in political activities.

Jane answered truthfully. She admitted she worked among Jews, explaining that was the very purpose of the Scottish Mission. She admitted she had wept when she had to send girls to school from the hostel wearing the yellow Star of David. She admitted she had dismissed her Aryan housekeeper, but claimed this was to meet the new racial prohibition on Aryans working in a house occupied by Jews. Jane claimed, moreover, that she had arranged a generous severance payment for the housekeeper/cook and helped her to find another job. She admitted to possessing a radio, but claimed she needed it to listen to air-raid warnings in order to try to protect her girls. (There was an air-raid shelter at the mission.) She argued it was natural for her – a Briton – to entertain British visitors. She admitted that she had visited British prisoners of war and sent them parcels, both of which she asserted the Hungarian government had given her permission to do. The only charge she denied was discussing – still less participating in – politics. This, she said, was completely false.

Both the Hungarian church and the Swiss Legation attempted to procure Jane's release, but without success. Bishop Ravasz even requested the Regent of Hungary, Miklós Horthy, to intervene, but the latter said he 'had no power to effect the release of the brave lady, so well-known in a wide circle by her generosity'. He was correct: Jane was the prisoner of the Germans, not of the Hungarian government. Yet the bishop's claims should perhaps be considered in the context of his pre-war votes in the Hungarian parliament's upper house in favour of anti-Semitic legislation. He had also made broadcasts in which he referred to Jews as strangers in Hungarian society, dominating the economy and the liberal professions. Such radio sermons helped translate anti-Jewish prejudice into theologically and intellectually acceptable anti-Semitism. The same bishop claimed 'mixing Gypsy and Hungarian blood is harmful', thereby stoking anti-Roma hostility.[5]

In late April Jane was transferred from Fö utca Prison to a holding camp at Kistarcsa, about 25 kilometres outside Budapest. 'After seventeen days in prison, she was taken away but left in very good health and spirits,' Frances Lee recalled. 'We all felt sure she was going to a pleasant outdoor camp. Little did I realize I would never see her again . . . She endeared herself to all her fellow-prisoners and everybody wept when she left.' Such optimism seems at odds with her guard's parting shot that she was being taken elsewhere 'since she loved the Jews so much'.

Around 12 May 1944 Jane was loaded into a railway cattle truck full of prisoners bound for Auschwitz-Birkenau. In the third week of her captivity friends arrived at Fö utca Prison bringing supplies, only to discover that she had vanished. No one could – or would – tell them where she had been taken. The deportees were now transported to the Slovak border on

---

5 Theo Tschry, *Dangerous Diplomacy: The story of Carl Lutz, rescuer of 62,000 Hungarian Jews*, Wm. B. Eerdmans, Grand Rapids, MI, 2000, pp. 116–17.

a Hungarian train, and then transferred to German wagons for the onward journey to southern Poland. Crowded into the wagons, with little air, light, food or water, and with buckets for latrines, many died during the journey.

Olga Lengyel, a Hungarian survivor of Auschwitz, described a similar journey:

> The cattle car had become an abattoir. More and more prayers for the dead rose in the stifling atmosphere. But the S.S. would neither let us bury nor remove them. We had to live with our corpses around us, the dead, the contagiously ill, those suffering from organic diseases, the parched, the famished and the mad.[6]

Gertrude Levi, also deported from Hungary to Auschwitz in 1944, described her journey as follows:

> The normal load for the trucks was 60–90 people, we were 120 . . . We had two buckets for our human needs, we had to overcome our inhibitions to use them – men, women, strangers, children . . . [W]ith every jolt of the train the muck ran out so we were sitting in it and couldn't do a thing about it. This was June 1944, a very hot summer, and there was little air in the truck. The two openings had barbed wire over them and the air became really unbearable . . . [W]e were getting thirstier and thirstier . . . you were hungry, you had a piece of bread in your hand but couldn't eat it because you couldn't swallow any

---

6 *Five Chimneys*, English translation, 1959.

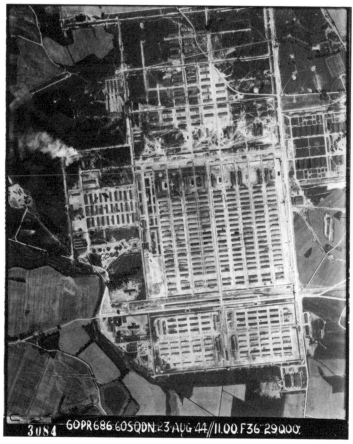

Aerial view of Auschwitz concentration camp taken from an RAF plane

Wiki commons

more. It meant people went into hysterics, people went mad, people had heart attacks and people died.

Jane arrived at Auschwitz on 15 May in a truck containing 31 Hungarian Jews. It seems that she was categorized as a 'political' prisoner: her alleged political activities had been the final accusation brought against her in Budapest. It has been claimed that some of Jane's Jewish pupils were sent with her to the camps. Ben Helfgott, a Holocaust survivor and Chair of the Yad Vashem Committee of the Board of Deputies of British Jews, claimed, 'When the children were taken away [Jane] went with them to Auschwitz. She was not able to save them, but she looked after them.' Certainly children and families Jane had known were taken to Auschwitz, and many perished there. A few somehow lived through this experience, including a mission school pupil named Judit Beck, the sole member of her family to survive the Holocaust.

From May 1944 trains arriving at Auschwitz II ran on a new rail spur, built to carry Hungarian Jews directly into the camp. The three-track line stopped close to the gas chambers, enabling a new train to arrive while the previous one was still being unloaded. The crematoria could scarcely cope, so the *Sonderkommando* (prisoners forced to work there) had to start burning bodies in open fire pits. In May 1944 360,000 people were killed at Auschwitz; in June 512,000; and between 1 and 26 July 442,000. In a little less than three months, more than 1,300,000 people were liquidated, most of them Hungarian Jews.

When prisoners arrived, guards immediately separated those to be taken directly to the gas chamber from those regarded as fit enough to undertake heavy manual work. Jane was in the latter minority, and, like every other concentration camp prisoner, was tattooed with a number, in her case 79467. Many of the women were sent to labour in the mines for 14 hours a day, with a food allowance of merely two bowls of thin soup. Olga Lengyel described the prisoners' living conditions:

> The roof was in deplorable repair. When it rained, the water leaked in and the internees on the top bunks were literally inundated . . . There was no floor except the beaten earth, dirty and wet, which the lightest rainfall turned into a sea of mud. Besides, at the lowest level the air was absolutely suffocating. The filth in the barrack surpassed imagination.

Despite the indescribable nature of the death camp, Jane was able to send two lettercards from Auschwitz. The last, written in German, was to her close friend Margit Prém in Budapest. Postmarked 'Auschwitz, Oberschlesien, 21 July 1944' – four days after her death – one side is headed *Konzentrationslager Auschwitz* (Auschwitz concentration camp) and lists the rules for corresponding with prisoners. Haining's name, date of birth and prisoner number were added in pencil in what appears to be her handwriting, and it was signed, as was her habit, 'Jean'. The other side is dated 15 July 1944, also in pencil. The letter mainly concerns the well-being of other people and practical details about life at the school, but also requests food.[7]

---

7 It seems that such censored communications formed part of a propaganda effort by the Nazi authorities to pretend that camp conditions were not oppressive and to conceal the true nature of the death camps.

My dearest Margit,

I have not yet had an answer to my first letter, but I know there is nothing you can do about that. I'll repeat it briefly, in case by any chance you haven't received it. You're allowed to write to me twice a month, and I'm allowed to write once a month, but only to you.

Parcels are not restricted by number or name [of the recipient]. I asked you to register me with our Red Cross, but also to send me a few parcels until the Red Cross can begin, but in addition I should like it if you could possibly send me apples or other fresh fruit and biscuits, rusks and other kinds of bread, as of course the Red Cross doesn't send things like that.

Margit, Margit, what are you thinking of doing with the flour? Are you going to sell it? What is upstairs is the best . . . but you know, ought one to sift through all that is left? Have you used up the eggs too?[8]

How are you all? I think of you day and night lovingly and longingly. I'm awaiting news of what everyone is doing, including your dear family, Margit. Is your old aunt still with us? . . . There's not much to report from here. Even here, on the way to heaven, [illegible] are mountains, but not as beautiful or as high as ours. I send appropriate greetings to the whole family and kiss and embrace you.

Your loving Jean.

---

8   Is it possible this paragraph bears a coded message, that eggs and flour stand for something other?

Maybe the reference to heaven implies that Jane knew she had little time to live. It has even been suggested that the 'way to heaven' (*Himmelstrasse*)[9] refers to the road leading to the gas chamber.

Not until June 1944 was the office of the Church of Scotland in George Street, Edinburgh informed that Jane had been arrested. Then on 2 August they were told she was in Auschwitz, and on 17 August they received a death certificate sent by the German Legation in Budapest via neutral Switzerland: 'Miss Haining, who was arrested on account of justified suspicion of espionage against Germany, died in hospital, July 17, of cachexia brought on by intestinal catarrh.'[10] This seems to bear out the view of the Edinburgh University historian Dr David Kaufman that Jane was arrested as an enemy national rather than specifically for her sympathy for the Jewish people.[11]

Jane Haining was 47 years old when she died at Auschwitz. Cachexia is a general collapse of the system due to insufficient food or chronic illness. Jane had undergone a second gall bladder operation in January 1944 and the harsh conditions at Auschwitz probably exacerbated her illness. Yet it is unlikely the stated cause of death was the true one; it is probable she

---

9 The word is almost indecipherable in the MS: it could be *Himmelsgang* (a Lutheran word for death and the passage to heaven of a Christian) or *Himmelsgrenze*, literally 'border of heaven', a compound word not otherwise known. *Himmelstrasse* was cynically used by Nazis at Sobibór death camp to refer to the way to the gas chamber.

10 The British politician Gordon Brown called this 'a gesture of quite surreal bureaucratic propriety considering the brutality of the regime, and one that bore no relation to the facts as subsequently established'. *Wartime Courage: Stories of extraordinary courage by ordinary people in World War Two*, Bloomsbury, London, 2008, p. 102.

11 Mary Miller, *Jane Haining: A life of love and courage*, Birlinn, Edinburgh, 2019, p. 203.

was killed in the gas chamber, along with many Hungarian women.

Less than a month later, on 14 August 1944, Jane's close friend Margit Prém died 'after becoming more and more melancholic after her best friend's departure', according to Louis Nagy. Her family believe she committed suicide, a belief reinforced by the fact that she died at a hospital known to specialize in caring for those who had attempted to take their own life.

A Gestapo operative delivered a parcel of Jane's possessions to the Scottish Mission in Budapest on 22 August 1944. It was found to contain a variety of items, including typed recipes for conserves, letters, a book of shopping lists and a twentieth-century English translation of the New Testament. In 2016 these personal effects were uncovered at the Church of Scotland's headquarters in Edinburgh. They also include Jane's handwritten will, dated 1942; more than 70 photographs of the Jewish girls she risked her life trying to protect; and a report by Bishop László Ravasz of his unsuccessful attempts to secure her release from prison:[12]

The Hungarian Reformed Church surrounded with sympathy and high esteem this frail and heroic-spirited lady. Her superiors had three times insisted on her to go home, but she had always declined. Twofold are our griefs: being ourselves captives, we were not able to save her; and being trodden down, we had no power to stand up for her more effectively.

---

12 Now in the National Library of Scotland.

One of the hostel girls wrote later describing how Jane Haining had comforted her when her mother first left her at the mission:

Suddenly I heard a nice voice, 'O you would be our little Anna.' I could not see anything except a couple of beautiful blue eyes and I felt a motherly kiss on my cheek. So this was my first meeting with Miss Haining, and from this very moment I loved her with all my heart . . . The days of horror were coming and Miss Haining protested against those who wanted to distinguish between one child of one race and the child of another . . . Then she was taken away. I still feel tears in my eyes and hear in my ears the siren of the Gestapo motor-car. I see the smile on her face when she bade me farewell . . . Letters were going and coming, at first frequently, later on, not so often, till they ceased and contact was broken off. I never saw Miss Haining again, and when I went to the Scottish Mission to ask the minister about her, I was told she had died. I did not want to believe it, nor to understand, but a long time later I realized that she had died for me and for others. The body of Miss Haining is dead, but she is still alive, because her smile, voice, face are still in my heart.

Ibolya Surányi agreed: 'She died because she cared for the life of others.' Four of Jane's former pupils have been filmed describing her efforts: Dr Zsuzanna Pajs, Dr Maria Kremer and Ibolya Surányi from Budapest and Annette Lantos from Washington DC.

In 1997, the centenary of Jane Haining's birth, Yad Vashem recognized her as one of the Righteous Among the Nations. She is also commemorated by a memorial cairn between the kirk and the graveyard in Dunscore, her native Scottish village, while a section of a main road along the River Danube in Budapest is named 'Jane Haining *rakpart*'. In January 2018 a heritage centre celebrating her 'heroism, bravery and personal sacrifice' was opened at Jane's home church in Dunscore.

The Scottish Mission – now St Columba's – still stands, at Vörösmarty utca 51, Budapest, having survived the Nazi occupation and use by the Russians as stables. After the war, Jane's Bible was discovered in the hostel and is now on display there. Most of the mission building is now a state school, but the church remains open for worship every Sunday.

4

No hiding place

CORRIE TEN BOOM, HAARLEM

Corrie ten Boom is probably the best-known 'righteous Gentile' of the Holocaust. Her books – especially *The Hiding Place* – have outsold almost every other book about the rescue of Jews during the Second World War. However, Corrie has often been neglected or ignored by academic Holocaust scholars, probably because she was in part motivated by Christian proselytization:

> Biographies such as that of Corrie ten Boom convey awareness of and sensitivity toward Jewish suffering and look upon the Jews amicably and appreciatively . . . as heirs to the Biblical covenant between Israel and God, [yet] the horrors they underwent during World War II are seen as footsteps in their collective spiritual pilgrimage towards recognizing the 'true' message of God.[1]

---

1 Yaakov Ariel, 'Jewish Suffering and Christian Salvation: The evangelical-fundamentalist memoirs', in *Holocaust and Genocide Studies*, Vol. 6, No. 1, 1991, p. 76.

Corrie – Cornelia Arnolda Johanna – ten Boom was born in the Jewish quarter of Amsterdam on 15 April 1892, the youngest of four children; her siblings were Betsie, Willem and Nollie. Her father, Casper, was a watchmaker and jeweller whose own father had in 1837 opened a shop in Haarlem in a house called the *Beje*, shortened from the street name, Barteljorisstraat.

Soon after Corrie's birth her grandfather died, so her family returned to Haarlem to run the shop, which consisted of two tall, narrow houses joined together. Corrie described it thus:

> The one in front was a typical tiny old-Haarlem structure, three stories high, two rooms deep and only one room wide. At some unknown point in its long history its rear wall had been knocked through to join it with the even thinner, steeper house behind it – which had only three rooms, one on top of the other – and this narrow corkscrew staircase squeezed between the two.[2]

The *Beje* was located in a Jewish neighbourhood and Corrie's grandfather had tried to nurture good Christian–Jewish relations. Corrie remembered 'in that narrow street in the ghetto [the family] met many wonderful Jewish people. They were allowed to participate in their Sabbaths and in their feasts. They studied the Old Testament together . . .' The family sympathized with the early Zionist settlers in Palestine,

---

2   Corrie ten Boom with John and Elizabeth Sherrill, *The Hiding Place*, Hodder & Stoughton, London, 1971, p. 8.

The ten Boom family home and watch shop in the *Beje*, Haarlem, today a museum
M. M. Minderhoud

viewing their activities as a sign that Christ's second coming was imminent.

When old enough, Corrie started helping her father in his shop. Finding her adept at the work, Casper sent his daughter to Switzerland to master the professional skill of watchmaking. In

Corrie ten Boom

1922 Corrie became the first Dutchwoman to obtain a watch-making licence.

After the First World War, the ten Boom family decided to help children in the defeated nation of Germany who were suffering badly from malnutrition, partly as a result of a lengthy economic blockade by the victorious Allies. Casper contacted fellow watchmakers across the Netherlands, asking them to take in one or two German children and feed them back to health before restoring them to their families at home. The ten Boom family took in four children.

Corrie's brother Willem studied theology at a seminary in Germany between 1927 and 1930. Several years before Hitler came to power he wrote a thesis on the threat of rising anti-Semitism in the German Weimar Republic, research that his professors derided. When Willem returned to the Netherlands, he ran a nursing home for the elderly of all faiths, which in the 1930s became a refuge for Jews fleeing Nazi Germany.

The ten Boom family belonged to the Calvinistic Dutch Reformed Church, which opposed the Nazi persecution of Jews as an injustice and an affront to God. In her auto-biography, *The Hiding Place*, Corrie set out her religious motives for hiding Jews, in particular her family's strong belief in the equality of human beings before God. Calvinist Christians tended to view Jews as religious kin, as both saw themselves as chosen by God. Other Dutch Reformed rescuers have said, 'We were brought up in a tradition in which we had learned that the Jewish people were the people of the Lord . . . The main reason [for rescue] is because we know that they are the chosen people of God. We had to save them.' Jews found among many Calvinist Christians a respect and solidarity *because* they were Jews, fellow believers in the God of Abraham and Moses; they viewed Jews as religious kin in a way most Christians do not. During the German occupation, the more fundamentalist Dutch Calvinist churches, which made up just 8 per cent of the population, were responsible for some 25 per cent of rescues of Jewish people.

Despite the Netherlands being a neutral country, Germany invaded without warning in late spring 1940. On 14 May the first large-scale airborne attack in the history of warfare was inflicted upon the citizens of Rotterdam, only 30 miles from the ten Boom family's home town of Haarlem. It was devastating. Five days later the Nazis threatened Holland with a second raid and the Dutch government surrendered.

Three-quarters of the Jews of the Netherlands were killed in the Holocaust: a greater proportion than in any other sizeable nation in Western Europe. Queen Wilhelmina was opposed to collaborating with the Germans, but the Dutch Prime Minister, Dirk Jan de Geer, believed his nation was unable to withstand the German army and so should cooperate with the Nazis, in much the same way as the Vichy government did in southern France.

Most Dutch civil servants helped the Germans administer their country. The Dutch government-in-exile, which opposed such action, explained how this happened: 'They [the civil service] had spent their whole lives accustomed to obey . . . they brought the same conscientiousness and the same fulfilment of duty to the scrupulous organization of the plunder of our country, to the advantage of the enemy.'[3] Almost every

---

3   Statement made in 1943.

government employee signed a form confirming that he or she was of 'Aryan' descent, and in November 1940 complied with German demands to purge Jews from public service. The Dutch civil service also facilitated German demands that every Jew be individually registered, which assisted the Nazis enormously when they started rounding up and deporting Dutch Jews to the death camps.

Though there had been anti-Semitic incidents in the Netherlands during the 1930s, the idea of persecuting the Jews ran counter to the tradition of Dutch tolerance that dated back to the end of the eighteenth century, and a philo-Semitic culture that grew up following the Reformation. A false sense of security led many to feel that the future could not be totally dark.

The German occupation brought many changes for all Dutch families. Every Dutch citizen had now to carry an identity card at all times. The Dutch police were placed under the direct control of the German authorities and could stop Dutch citizens at any time and demand to see their identity card, which was supposed to be carried in a pouch hung from the neck. Telephones could be cut off and bicycles confiscated, and everyone needed a ration card to buy food. The Nazis also demanded that all radios be handed over. The ten Booms had two sets: they handed one in, but hid the second under the stairs so they could continue listen to BBC news reports about the war.

For the Jews, life was much more heavily restricted. By June 1941 a wide range of anti-Semitic measures had been put in place. Jews could no longer visit cinemas, public parks or swimming pools, possess a car, attend a mixed school, or work as a lawyer or doctor for anyone except Jewish clients. Shops now displayed signs saying 'JEWS WILL NOT BE SERVED' and public parks, libraries and concert halls put up notices at their entrances saying 'No JEWS'. Stirred up by the pro-Nazi National Socialist Bond, people threw stones and bricks at Jewish-owned businesses and smeared anti-Semitic slogans on synagogues. Jewish shops closed down and Jewish homes emptied.

Things soon became even worse. Dutch Jews were now made to wear the yellow Star of David on their clothing. To show he identified with them, Corrie's father, 80-year-old Casper ten Boom, apparently went to Haarlem's town hall with Jewish citizens to obtain a yellow star himself. When his daughters remonstrated, he replied, 'If God's people must suffer then I will suffer.' With difficulty, they persuaded him that this gesture, however laudable, wouldn't help his Jewish friends but could create unnecessary new problems.

Corrie's family soon became actively involved in the Dutch resistance movement. Since the start of the occupation, her brother Willem had been hiding Jews in his home and elsewhere. For their own safety, he moved the younger Jews out of his nursing home, but thought the older residents could remain unharmed. Not all were so optimistic: the rabbi of Haarlem had already brought his library of antiquarian Jewish theology books to the *Beje* for safekeeping 'in case I should not be able to care for them'. He was among the first Jews of Haarlem to disappear.

In November 1941 Corrie watched helplessly as four Germans stole fur coats from the shop owned by their Jewish neighbour, Mr Weil. The thieves then set about smashing up his premises. Corrie and Betsie took Weil into their home until Willem's son Kik could take him to safety with his wife.

The following May a woman called Mrs Kleermaker came to the door of the *Beje* carrying a little suitcase. She explained that she was Jewish, her husband had been arrested several months earlier, and her son was in hiding. The previous day agents from the *Sicherheitsdienst* (the intelligence-gathering arm of the SS and the Nazi Party) had ordered her to close down her clothes shop, so she was too scared to return to her flat over the premises. She had heard that the ten Booms had helped the Weils and hoped they would help her too. Casper ten Boom invited her to stay with them, although a police station stood almost opposite their house. 'In this household, God's people are always welcome,' he told their visitor. Two nights later another elderly Jewish couple came looking for refuge.

The ten Booms were not alone in this work. Only four doors along from the *Beje*, a Dutchwoman named de Boer was hiding 18 Jewish fugitives in her attic, most of them quite young. Possibly stir-crazy, eight of them ventured out one night and were quickly arrested. They soon divulged where they had been hiding, and Mrs de Boer and the rest of her guests were all taken too.

The three ten Booms living at the *Beje* – Corrie, her father, Casper, and sister Betsie – now agreed to conceal Jews in their home on a regular basis. Corrie had begun to recognise the possible cost: working with the resistance might mean lying, stealing, perhaps even killing, and struggled to reconcile this with her strong Christian principles. 'If a Nazi comes to the door and asks, "Do you have Jews here?"' she said, 'naturally I will lie.' When an official asked if the radio she had turned in was the only one the family possessed, Corrie lied by saying 'Yes'. 'I had known from childhood that the earth opened and the heavens rained fire upon liars,' she wrote later. But she began to tremble 'not because for the first time in my life I had told a conscious lie. But because it had been so dreadfully easy.'[4] For a family devoted to truth-telling as part of their Christian value system, such behaviour was difficult to justify, and on occasion led to sharp differences between them over what they did and said. In due course Corrie was arrested and sent to a concentration camp, but never did she reveal the location of the family's secret hiding place or admit she had helped fugitive Jews.

A young Christian resistance worker named Johannes (Hans) Poley (1924–2003) found shelter in their home. 'Their love for God's chosen people made the ten Booms respect . . . the convictions of the Jews they sheltered,' he wrote later. 'They never abused the integrity of their guests by attempting to convert them. They had many animated discussions, but considered their daily life to be sufficient example of their faith in Christ.' Between June and December 1943, while hiding at the *Beje*, Poley took a number of photographs with a box camera of others in hiding. Poley was later arrested for his resistance activities and sent to Amersfoort concentration camp.

One unforgettable Jewish fugitive concealed for months by the ten Booms was the irrepressible *chazzan* (cantor) of the Jewish community in Amsterdam, Meijer Mossel, who was given the distinctive fake identity of 'Eusebius Smit', or 'Eusie' for short. When he asked permission to say his prayers and sing in their home, the ten Booms assented – but warned that

---

4   ten Boom, *The Hiding Place*, p. 66.

he wouldn't be able to eat according to strict kosher rules as the utensils in the house weren't ritually clean. 'Should I starve and die, or eat non-kosher and live to praise my Lord?' he replied. 'Your food will be my pleasure!' A Jewish woman named Mary van Itallie, whose parents had committed suicide to avoid deportation, also found refuge in the *Beje*.

Other Dutch Christians were much less willing to help Jews in need. On one occasion Corrie asked a visiting pastor to help her protect a mother and her newborn child. 'Certainly not!' he replied. 'We could lose our lives for that Jewish child.' Old Casper overheard him. 'Give the child to me, Corrie,' he said. 'You say we could lose our lives for this child. I would consider that the greatest honour that could come to my family.' This story did not have a happy ending. The ten Booms arranged for the mother and her baby to be taken for safety to a market gardener on the outskirts of Haarlem. But the Gestapo raided the farm soon after, discovered the fugitives in a barn and took them both away, together with the farmer who had concealed them.

The ten Boom shop soon became a focus of underground activity. Corrie hid ration cards in a stairwell and constructed a secret hiding place for fugitives. Scores of Jews passed through the house, staying for anything from a single night to several weeks. Corrie and Betsie managed to get their cut-off telephone line reinstalled, which was vital as Corrie tried to co-ordinate a team of up to 80 underground helpers. The two sisters developed their own code for talking confidentially on the phone, all too aware it might be tapped. For example: 'We have a woman's watch here that needs repairing. I can't find a mainspring. Do you know who might have one?' meant: 'We have a Jewish woman who needs a hiding place, but we can't find one among our regular contacts.'

Two years into the occupation, food became extremely scarce. Jews were not allocated ration cards by the authorities, so the ten Booms had to use their own to buy food for their Jewish guests. When this proved insufficient, a man whose disabled daughter Corrie had helped, and who worked at the local ration-card office, provided her with dozens of extra cards for the Jews she was helping. Sometimes Corrie had to arrange medical care for hidden Jews, and she even organized a burial in a Christian cemetery for a Jew who had died.

In Corrie's bedroom on the top floor of the *Beje* a secret room was constructed, where Jews and resistance workers could hide if the Gestapo raided. The fact that the building consisted of two joined houses with different floor levels made it easier to conceal this hiding place. When neighbours noticed building materials being taken into the house, Betsie told them, 'We've been here a long time and need some modern facilities' – letting them think the family were adding a new bathroom.

A cupboard with a false wall was quickly constructed. At the back of the cupboard was a moveable panel about three feet wide and two feet high, which slid in tight grooves so that no slits were visible when it was shut. A cord passed over a wheel, while a counterweight helped the panel slide smoothly. Once Corrie had rehung her clothes in the cupboard there was nothing to indicate there was a secret space behind the wall. Six or seven people could stand upright in *de Schuilplaats* (the hiding place), which was fitted out with a mattress, a bucket of water, vitamins and dry biscuits. When the ten Booms began taking in more permanent guests, they installed an alarm to be sounded in the event of a police raid. Corrie insisted that visitors practise repeatedly getting themselves and their belongings into the hiding place – which they nicknamed the 'angels' crib' – till they could do so in less than 90 seconds.

On Saturday 14 August 1943 Corrie's sister Nollie, who lived elsewhere in Haarlem, was arrested and taken to the Gestapo headquarters for interrogation. Annaliese, the Jewish girl she had been sheltering, was sent to the Department for Jewish Affairs, the *Judenstelle*, in Amsterdam, where she was held in an old Jewish theatre until a raid by the Resistance freed her and 40 other prisoners. Nollie was detained in prison in Amsterdam for seven weeks. Things had now become so dangerous that the ten Booms decided that their guests had to leave.

On Monday 28 February 1944 a stranger came into their shop, insisting he must speak to Corrie. He proceeded to tell her a story about his wife having been arrested in the town of Alkmaar, and how he could obtain her release if he paid 600 Dutch guilders. He was unable to give a single name as a reference to prove he was trustworthy. Although there was every reason to suspect him of being an informer, Corrie told him to return in the afternoon, by which time she said she would have found the money.

The Gestapo raided the same day. They searched the entire house and uncovered the hiding place under the stairs containing ration cards, savings, watches and the possessions of Jewish families who had been arrested or were in hiding. As the search proceeded, the leader of the raid took Corrie and Betsie into the watch repair shop and interrogated them roughly. He hit Corrie across the face several times in an attempt to make her reveal the location of the secret room. Finally he arrested both sisters for the crime of helping Jewish people, *Judenhilfe*. Corrie, her father, Casper, her brother, Willem, her sisters Betsie and Nollie, and Nollie's son Peter were all taken to the police station, together with 35 others who had been recorded entering the house that day, some for a prayer meeting in the living room. At the police station the prisoners managed to flush down the toilet a number of incriminating items.

From the police station in Haarlem they were taken to the Gestapo headquarters in The Hague for interrogation, and then by lorry to the penitentiary in the nearby seaside town of Scheveningen. All but Corrie, Betsie and father ten Boom were soon released.

When a guard asked old Casper ten Boom if he realized he could die for protecting Jews, he replied, 'It would be an honour to give my life for God's ancient people.' Sadly, his mind soon began to wander; brutal prison life and malnutrition rapidly broke his fragile health. Casper was transferred unconscious to Ramar Clinic, where on 9 March he died alone on a stretcher in a corridor, aged 84. He was buried in an unmarked grave. After the war the site was identified and he was reburied in the Erebegraafplaats Bloemendaal, the Dutch National Field of Honour at Loenen, near the town of Apeldoorn.

Throughout the raid on the *Beje* six people – both Jews and resistance workers – had been hiding in the secret place behind the cupboard. They remained concealed for two days, with neither food nor water, until convinced the Gestapo had ended their surveillance of the house. Four days after the raid, resistance workers moved the fugitives to new locations; all but one survived the war. In custody, Corrie ten Boom received a coded message: 'All the watches in your cupboard are safe' – meaning that all the fugitives had escaped and were safe.

Corrie was initially held in solitary confinement. Then, after three months, came her first court hearing. As part of her defence, Corrie described the work she had been engaged in previously, helping the mentally disabled. This was summarily dismissed; justifying it by their eugenics ideology, Nazis had been killing the mentally ill for years. Corrie ten Boom responded by asserting that in God's eyes a disabled person might be more valuable 'than a watchmaker . . . or a lieutenant . . .' After thorough investigation she signed a protocol of her evidence, which concluded:

> She plans to continue in the future what she has done in the past, because she wants to help all those who appeal to her for aid, regardless of their race or creed. She is determined to do this because she is obedient to the command of Christ to love God and her neighbours.[5]

Corrie and Betsie were both held at Scheveningen until 8 June 1944, when they were transported to Kamp Vught, an internment camp near Herzogenbusch. Betsie was tattooed with prisoner number 66729, Corrie with number 66730. At this camp Betsie was forced to sew prison uniforms, while Corrie had to assemble radios for the Dutch electronics company Philips for installation in Luftwaffe warplanes. A fellow

---

5 Corrie ten Boom, *A Prisoner and Yet*, Chipmunk Books, CLC, Fort Washington, PA, 1971, p. 40.

prisoner told her to slow down and deliberately sabotage her work to avoid giving unnecessary support to the German war effort.

Early in September the Germans executed some 700 male prisoners at Kamp Vught; Betsie and Corrie heard the shooting. The following day, both sisters were jammed into a single goods wagon along with 80 other women, who were screaming, crying and fainting upright owing to the intense pressure of bodies. The train moved in fits and starts, taking all of four days to transport the prisoners to Ravensbrück, the concentration camp for women in north Germany.

When at last they arrived, the women spent their first two nights sleeping in the rain in a field. Then Corrie was allocated to Barracks 28, where around 1,400 women were crammed into a building built to house just 400. At morning roll-call each day they had to stand for hours without moving, while smoke from the crematorium chimneys reminded them constantly that men and women were dying nearby.

Roused each day at 4 a.m., Corrie, Betsie and thousands of other women prisoners had to walk a mile and a half to the huge Siemens factory, where they were forced to labour for hours, unloading heavy metal plates from railway goods wagons and wheeling them by handcart to the factory gate. At lunchtime they were allotted a boiled potato and thin soup; those left at the camp had no midday meal at all. It was utterly exhausting work for women in their fifties, yet when they returned to the camp, Betsie and Corrie held services. Somehow Corrie had managed to smuggle her Bible into the camp. 'A meeting might include a recital of the Magnificat in Latin by a group of Roman Catholics,' Corrie recalled, 'a whispered

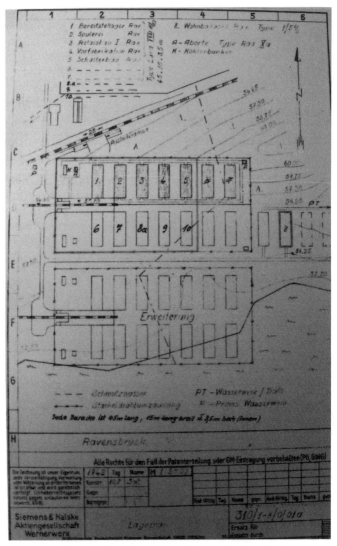

Plan of the Siemens work camp barracks,
Ravensbrück concentration camp, Brandenburg, Germany

Wiki commons

hymn by some Lutherans and a *sotto voce* chant by Eastern Orthodox women.'

On one occasion, Corrie discovered she had been scheduled to work at a munitions factory elsewhere, so she deliberately failed an eye test in order to stay at Ravensbrück, close to her ailing sister Betsie. The two sisters managed to remain together until Betsie, who had for years suffered from pernicious anaemia, died on 16 December 1944, aged 59.

Later the same month, apparently as the result of an administrative error, Corrie was released from Ravensbrück, receiving a discharge certificate on Christmas Eve. She was unable to leave immediately, however: a camp doctor diagnosed oedema in her feet and ankles and ordered her to be admitted to the camp hospital. On New Year's Day 1945 Corrie ten Boom was finally declared fit to leave.

With other released prisoners, Corrie was taken by train first to Berlin and then on to Groningen in the Netherlands, where she spent a further ten days convalescing in hospital. A lorry then transported her to Willem's home in Hilversum, and finally back to the *Beje*. She discovered that Willem's son Kik had been taken to Bergen-Belsen concentration camp the previous year. When the camp was liberated by the Russian army, Kik was sent with the other prisoners to a labour camp in Russia, where he died aged only 24.

Corrie ten Boom returned home in the midst of the 'hunger winter' (*Hongerwinter*), the appalling Dutch famine of the winter of 1944–5 largely caused by a German blockade preventing vital supplies of food and fuel from getting through. In May 1945 she rented a 56-room residence called Schapendunien in Bloemendaal and converted it to house the mentally disabled

Konzentrationslager _____ Ravensbrück _____

Kommandantur

IV/ 6673o/Bo/Hö.

Ravensbrück, den 28.12.44

Entlassungsschein

Cornelis A.J. ten B o o m

Der Häftling _____ 15.4.92 _____ in _____ Amsterdam _____ hat vom _____ 8.9.44 _____

geb. am _____ im Konzentrationslager eingewiesen.

bis zum heutigen Tage im Konzentrationslager eingewiesen.

Ihm wurde aufgegeben, sich bis auf Widerruf jeden _____ Werktag bei der Ortspolizeibehörde seines

Wohnortes sofort bei m. Meldebehörde der Sipo.u.d.SD.,Den Haag in Rotterdam/
Hannover

zu melden.

Der Häftling war hier polizeilich nicht gemeldet. / Lebensmittel, Kleider- und Volkskarteikarten

sind für die Dauer des Aufenthaltes in dem Konzentrationslager nicht ausgeteilt worden

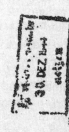

Der _____ Kommandant

SS-Sturmbannführer u.Kdt.

30. DEZ 1944

and provide space for prisoners liberated from concentration camps to recover from their traumas. When peace came, she pressed for reconciliation to help heal the psychological scars inflicted by the Nazi occupation.

In the years that followed, Corrie ten Boom travelled widely as a Christian evangelist and motivational speaker, recounting her experiences in Ravensbrück and offering support to prisoners. In 1977 she moved to Placentia, California, where she died on her ninety-first birthday. In all the ten Boom family helped conceal around 80 Jewish people during the Second World War. Corrie was knighted by the Dutch queen in 1962, and on 12 December 1967 she was invited to plant a tree in Yad Vashem's Avenue of the Righteous Gentiles.

The ten Boom house in Haarlem, the *Beje*, is now a museum, where the wall in Corrie's old bedroom has been cut open so that visitors can look into the hiding place.

5

Quakers and U-boats

DR ELISABETH ABEGG, BERLIN

How the Quaker Elisabeth Abegg avoided arrest by the Nazis is a mystery. Because of her anti-Nazi opinions, she was twice forced to leave a Berlin school where she was teaching. She refused to fly the swastika from her flat despite neighbours' complaints. Over the last three years of the war she concealed in her small flat 12 Jewish fugitives. And she was at the hub of a busy network of people who hid as many as 80 Jews attempting to evade detection by the Nazi authorities. Yet she was never caught.

Elisabeth Abegg was born on 3 March 1882 in Strasbourg, Alsace (now part of France), at a time when it was a province of the German Reich. In 1912 she enrolled at Leipzig University to study history, classics and Romance languages, one of the first German women to be admitted to university education. While at university she took a factory job to support her and to experience something of the life of a working woman. Graduating with a doctorate in medieval history in 1916, she published her thesis on medieval Milan.[1] Elisabeth knew, and was much influenced by the teachings of, another native of Alsace, the celebrated Dr Albert Schweitzer (1875–1965), musician, theologian, humanist and medical doctor. When France reclaimed the disputed border territory of Alsace under the peace settlement following the First World War, Elisabeth moved to Berlin and assisted Quakers in their post-war relief work, providing much-needed food and medical support.[2]

An advocate of women's rights, Dr Abegg was appointed in 1924 to teach history, Latin and French at the prestigious Luisen-Oberlyzeum in Berlin's Mitte district, a girls' high school with social-democratic sympathies, many of whose pupils came from Jewish families. Elisabeth joined several left-leaning groups including the German Women's Association (*Allgemeine Deutsche Frauenverein*) and the East Berlin Social Workers' Association, set up to support disadvantaged young women by Friedrich Siegmund-Schultze (1885–1969), a Protestant minister committed to social justice and international reconciliation, and one of the first pastors to suffer persecution by the Nazis.

Dr Abegg freely expressed her humanistic beliefs, centred on the sanctity of human life, and when Adolf Hitler assumed power in 1933 she began to criticize the Nazi regime. By the mid-1930s she was in contact with a resistance organization centred on Hans Robinsohn (1897–1981) and Ernst Strassmann (1897–1958), which was making significant efforts to support oppressed Jews. Along with fellow teachers

---

1 *Die Politik Mailands in den ersten Jahrzeiten des 13 Jahrhunderts.*

2 For details of this work, see Joan Mary Fry, *In Downcast Germany 1919–1933*, James Clark, London, 1944.

and some older students at the Luisen-Oberlyzeum, such as Hildegard Knies (1915–97), Elisabeth opposed Nazi measures at the school and discrimination against its Jewish students.

Before long such activities brought Elisabeth to the attention of the new Nazi-appointed director of the school. She was disciplined for criticizing significant figures in German history such as Frederick the Great and Otto von Bismarck, the 'Iron Chancellor', and in 1935 was forced to move to the Rückert-Gymnasium in Berlin's Bavaria district, where many Jewish families lived. By the end of the 1935–6 academic year, 120 Jewish pupils had been forced out, leaving only eight at the school. Dr Abegg was questioned by the Gestapo in 1938 regarding her support for a dissident theologian, and in 1941 she was forced into premature retirement after pupils and parents denounced her for claiming that British soldiers were as brave as Germans, for encouraging reconciliation and for refusing to take the Führer loyalty oath. In the same year she joined the Religious Society of Friends, the Quakers, although she had been active among them since 1940.[3]

During the 1930s German Jews suffered a systematic loss of their human rights. By 1939, with persecution and degradation the norm, they possessed no legal or moral protection. From January 1940, Jews were denied milk, fish, chicken, rice, cocoa and other staple foods. Recognizing the extent of oppression, some Quakers in Berlin had founded a youth group for

---

3 Although the Quakers were helping Jews to emigrate, and later hiding them from their Nazi persecutors, in 1932 there was heated debate in the Berlin Quaker meeting over whether the clerk, 'P.H.', who came from a Jewish family, could continue to hold this position: 'After much discussion and some resignations of members, the group decided that such distinctions could find no place in a body of friends.' 'P.H.' resigned in 1935. Fry, *In Downcast Germany 1919–1933*, p. 141.

outcasts in 1935 and started to campaign on behalf of concentration camp inmates. After 1937 they increased efforts to help Jews emigrate. With English and American Friends, the small Quaker community in Berlin set up its own relief centre, primarily for those who belonged neither to a Jewish organization nor to a church. On 11 April 1938 Quakers in a number of German cities protested against the Nazi-instigated boycott of Jewish businesses.

Although identified by the authorities as politically suspect, Abegg maintained contact with her Jewish friends and former students. The opposition group started when she was at the Luisen-Oberlyzeum remained active and included Hildegard Knies, now studying psychology in Berlin, and the father of another former pupil, a lawyer named Richard Linde. The dissident group met at Linde's home in Hohen Neuendorf, north of Berlin, to discuss politics and listen to the BBC news. From 1942 they began hearing about the crimes in the occupied territories, which strengthened their resolve to save those suffering persecution.

In September 1941 all Jews in the German Reich were ordered to wear the yellow Star of David. By this date many had already fled Germany; those remaining were forced into slave labour or deported to the eastern territories. On 15 October 1941 the Nazis started to deport German Jews to Poland and Latvia for 'resettlement' in so-called 'work camps', starting mainly with older men and women. One week later the German frontiers were closed to Jews, putting an end to emigration; Hitler was determined to prevent news of what he was perpetrating from leaking out. All remaining Jews were now to be sent to concentration camps.

Within a year, sealed trains were transporting between 1,000 and 1,500 Berlin Jews to the east every month. The elderly, war veterans and their families, and Jewish religious leaders and administrators were often sent initially to Theresienstadt (Terezín), a ghetto-like transit camp in Bohemia, which the Nazis maintained as a 'showcase' for the Red Cross to inspect. But most Berlin deportees were sent straight to Auschwitz-Birkenau, where the gas chambers were now fully operational, killing up to 10,000 Jews a day. Healthy men and some fit women were assigned to work duties; elderly and sick men, most women and almost all children were sent straight to the 'showers', where crystals of a cyanide gas called Zyklon B killed them within minutes. Much of the German population suspected what was going on. News of the gassings was restricted, but from an early stage soldiers and railway workers were telling stories of deaths and strange smells in the camps that passed back into the Jewish community. It has been estimated that around 7,000 Jews committed suicide in Berlin alone largely for fear of what awaited them in the East.

Many Berlin Jews went underground to escape the Nazis, having heard these alarming rumours from Gentile friends, acquaintances or strangers. They removed the yellow star from their clothing, destroyed or hid their ID documents and attempted to leave no trace of their existence. They sometimes left a 'suicide note' in an attempt to explain their disappearance and put the Gestapo off their trail, and often called themselves 'U-boats' in self-mocking reference to German submarines. The comparison was apt as well as sardonic: to survive 'underground' called for the wiles, stealth and courage of a submariner.

Part of Terezín (Theresienstadt) concentration camp, Bohemia, with the infamous motto *Arbeit macht frei* ('Work sets [you] free')

Wiki commons: Andrew Shiva

Those who attempted to protect these fugitive Jews were acting on individual initiative, sometimes on impulse, with little organized leadership, support or direction. As a result, most of the Jews in hiding were isolated from one another, as were most protectors from other protectors, rendering it difficult for the Gestapo to track them down easily or quickly. A self-contained 'cell' structure developed, which maximized secrecy – a structure similar to that frequently employed by spies and terror organizations. To uncover Jewish 'U-boats' the German authorities had to rely largely on reports from informers – sometimes fellow Jews – and unfriendly neighbours, who might report strange noises in nearby houses or spot Jewish acquaintances in the street.

Some Jews who went underground remained hidden throughout the war, but most – again like submarines – had constantly to surface and creep around, anxious that the Gestapo and SS might be on their trail or that neighbours would denounce them. They supported each other with hints, addresses of friendly individuals and warnings, a flow of information they called *Mundfunk*, or 'word of mouth' – a pun on *Rundfunk*, German for radio. Those who sheltered Jews were equally nervous and cautious: harbouring them could result in prison sentences of up to ten years. This unease meant that Jewish 'U-boats' often needed to find new hiding places within weeks – even days; rarely could they stay long in a safe 'haven'. They also had to find money for food and obtain the ration cards that would permit them legally to buy food – or otherwise develop black-market contacts.

Anna Hirschberg (1881–1944), a Protestant Christian of Jewish origin, had been Elisabeth's close friend for 40 years.

She had obtained a doctorate at the University of Greifswald in 1919 and worked in education, but was dismissed in 1933 because of her Jewish background and after 1939 failed to get a job at a Jewish school because of her adopted Christian faith. Now aged over 60 and with a worsening eye disease, Hirschberg turned down Abegg's offer to conceal and protect her in Berlin as she felt she couldn't cope with living as an 'illegal' U-boat. On 10 July 1942 Anna was deported to Terezín, and then on 16 May 1944 sent to Auschwitz, where in due course she was recorded as 'missing'. Anna's deportation brought home forcibly to Dr Abegg the reality of the Nazi persecution of the Jews. She resolved henceforth to do all she could to save others from her friend's fate. Years later Elisabeth Abegg learned that Anna Hirschberg had been murdered in Auschwitz in 1944.

Despite being the carer for her invalid older sister Julie and their 86-year-old bedridden mother, both of whom lived with her in a four-room flat at Berliner Strasse 24A[4] in Berlin's Tempelhof district, Dr Abegg now started to help Jews find safe shelter. She gradually built up an extensive rescue network of friends and former students to help, based around the Linde/ Knies group of her Luisen-Oberlyzeum days. A number of 'U-boats' sheltered in her flat or in nearby flats temporarily left empty. As the Allied bombing of Berlin grew heavier, two of Elisabeth's neighbours moved out of Berlin and left her the keys to their flats, which she was able to use as hiding places for U-boats. On one occasion a German soldier unexpectedly home on leave entered one of these flats and found a stranger

---

4   Today Tempelhofer Damm 56. The site is marked with a plaque.

in his family home: fortunately he didn't realize it was a Jewish fugitive.

Most of those who knocked at Dr Abegg's door asking for help were complete strangers, but she never hesitated to respond, despite some neighbours being active Nazis who suspected her of disloyalty, particularly as she refused to fly the swastika from her flat. Dr Abegg regularly provided meals for people living 'underground' and helped them financially, obtaining forged documents and teaching some of the children who were in hiding.

Among the first to find protection at Abegg's home was a Jewish nursery school teacher named Liselotte Pereles (1906–70) and her young foster-daughter, Susanne Manasse. Pereles had been a director of the Pestalozzi-Fröbel-Haus, a pioneering training centre for kindergarten teachers, but was forced to leave in 1933 at the very beginning of the Nazi era. From 1934 she was in charge of a Jewish after-school centre in the Kreuzberg district of Berlin. Living with her was nine-year-old Susanne, whose mother had died and whose father had fled to Shanghai in 1939 following detention in a Nazi concentration camp. Around New Year 1943 a friend introduced Pereles to Elisabeth Abegg, who offered to hide her and her foster-daughter.

In Berlin the Gestapo planned a massive raid, known as the 'Factory Action', on 27 February. The Berlin journalist Ruth Andreas-Friedrich graphically described what she witnessed:

Since six o'clock this morning trucks have been driving through Berlin, escorted by armed SS men. They stop at factory gates, in front of private houses; they load in human cargo – men, women, children. Distracted faces are crowded together under the grey canvas covers. Figures of misery, penned in and jostled about like cattle going to the stock-yards. More and more new ones arrive, and are thrust into the overcrowded trucks with blows of gun butts. In six weeks Germany is to be 'Jew-free'.

Following this mass raid, conducted by the Gestapo and Waffen-SS with lightning speed and extreme brutality, some 7,000 people were deported east in five transports. But this so-called 'Factory Action' was too big an operation to be kept completely secret and it acted as the final signal for many Jews to go into hiding. More than 4,000 Jews escaped the raid, often with children or relatives, and went into hiding in the city.

The children from the care centre and most of Liselotte's colleagues had already been deported when she heard of the 'Action'. She herself was arrested on 1 February but managed to escape from the holding centre. Using a previously agreed code, she phoned Elisabeth Abegg from Charlottenburg Station, telling her she had decided to go 'underground'. Elisabeth replied, 'Say hello to my friend from the "Ferdinand",' an instruction Liselotte understood to mean she should take Susanne to the empty flat of a friend of Elisabeth who was in hospital. There Liselotte hid with another Jewish woman, Steffi Collm,[5] while Elisabeth arranged for another Jewish fugitive, Anita Schäfer, to take them both food.

Liselotte now had to move frequently, hiding in turn with Hildegard Knies in Berlin-Charlottenburg, with Elisabeth

---

5   See below, pp. 138–9.

Abegg herself, and in the flat that Abegg's former RE teacher colleague Elisabeth Schmitz shared with her friend and former pupil Lydia Forsström (1914–2006). Both Schmitz and Forsström were devout Protestants who belonged to the Confessing Church.[6] When Schmitz moved out of Berlin to avoid the increasingly dangerous Allied air raids, Forsström continued sharing the flat with Pereles and helped her obtain a provisional ID card in the assumed name of 'Lilo Koch'. Lydia Forsström then accompanied 'Lilo' and Susanne to greater safety at the Alsace home of another in Abegg's circle, a Catholic seamstress named Margrit Dobbeck (1897–1951), who had been living in Schöneberg, Berlin.

Because she was of school age, Liselotte's ward Susanne was in particular danger of being discovered, so had to be moved on frequently. She spent some months hiding with her Gentile aunt Bertha Becker, who ran a grocer's shop in Lindow, near Neuruppin, north of Berlin. Ruth Wendland, another of Abegg's friends,[7] provided Susanne with a forged baptismal certificate and took her to stay with Dorothea Thiel, a pastor's wife in Gebersdorf, Brandenburg. Friends somehow got hold of a Nazi girls' association (*Bund Deutscher Mädel*) uniform

---

6　In 1933, pro-Nazi Protestant church leaders tried to force from pulpits 'non-Aryan clergy' – converts from Judaism to Christianity. To challenge this, the popular pastor Martin Niemöller (1892–1984) organized the Pastors' Emergency League, which evolved into the *Bekennende Kirche* (Confessing Church) movement and struggled for control with the *Deutsche Christen* ('German Christians'), who synthesized Protestant theology with Nazi ideology. But members of both camps tended to accept anti-Jewish dogma, and even Niemöller remained convinced until after the war that Germany suffered from a 'Jewish problem', and described the history of Jewish suffering as punishment for crucifying Jesus. Only a minority of German Protestants saw respect for Jews and Judaism as integral to authentic Christianity.

7　See below, p. 141.

for Susanne to wear as a disguise when she was travelling around Germany.

Several 'U-boat' Jews were welcomed at Richard Linde's home in Hohen Neuendorf, including Herta and Evy Goldstein and Eva Fleischmann, as well as forced labourers on the run and prisoners of war. Linde practised organic fruit and vegetable gardening and bee-keeping, so those hiding with him were well provided for. Linde's married daughter, Ruth-Maria Heiliger, who lived in an annexe to his house, and his gardener, Else Rückborn, both supported his relief efforts.

Linde employed as his legal assistant a Jewish woman named Margarete Hartmann (1893–1976), who continued to work for him unofficially after the Nazis had banned Jews from law offices. Hartmann was active in the political resistance, transcribing news from foreign radio stations and surreptitiously leaving duplicated copies in public places. When her activities were detected by the Nazis in the autumn of 1943 she went into hiding with friends, including Linde and Hildegard Knies.

The seamstress Margrit Dobbeck met Elisabeth Abegg through a Jewish dressmaker named Hertha Blumenthal, who was threatened with deportation and whom both supported when she went underground. At Abegg's request, in July 1943 Margrit's neighbour Philipp Schmitt took in a Jewish couple called Gertrud and Emil Stargardter, who had owned a department store in Glogau, Silesia (now Głogów, Poland), which had been expropriated in 1935. Dobbeck and Schmitt sometimes hid as many as seven people in their two flats, until neighbours realized what they were doing and Margrit had to return to her home in Mulhouse, Alsace, in autumn 1943.

Schmitt subsequently took several Berlin 'U-boats' to Dobbeck in Mulhouse, including Hertha Blumenthal, Flora Wolff and the Stargardters.

Elisabeth Abegg and her circle also concealed Jizchak Schwersenz (1915–2005), a Berlin Jew who finally escaped to Switzerland with their aid.[8] A trained teacher, Schwersenz[9] had been preparing teenagers in the Youth Aliyah Zionist organization for emigration to Palestine. In August 1942, hearing that he was about to be deported, he went underground as an 'illegal', ripping off his yellow star and replacing it with a swastika. An educator called Margarete Fränkel put Schwersenz in touch with Elisabeth Abegg, who referred him to Bertha Gerhardt, a Protestant Christian and school principal who had lost her job on political grounds. Gerhardt hid him in her home in Zepernick, on the outskirts of Berlin, and referred him on to Luise Meier, who had helped a number of Jews escape across the Swiss border. Dr Abegg gave Jizchak a ring to help pay helpers in southern Germany. Schwersenz obtained a passport forged by the Jewish graphic artist Samson 'Cioma' Schönhaus (1922–2015),[10] and with this successfully crossed into Switzerland on 13 February 1944.

---

8   For the full story of Jizchak Schwersenz, see Beate Meyer, Hermann Simon and Chana Schütz, eds, *Jews in Nazi Berlin: From Kristallnacht to liberation*, University of Chicago Press, Chicago and London, 2009, pp. 134–6, 138–9, 278–9.

9   His given names were Heinz Joachim.

10   Samson 'Cioma' Schönhaus, born in 1922 in Berlin, was forced to leave secondary school and his training as a graphic artist and made to work in the uniform and arms industry in Berlin. He used his skill to forge ID cards for 'U-boats', setting up a print shop with the Jewish printer Ludwig Lichtwitz. From September 1942 he went into hiding with a false identity and in October 1943 fled by bicycle to southern Germany before also crossing into Switzerland. His memoir *The Forger*, translated by Alan Bance, was published by Granta Books, London, 2007.

Elisabeth Abegg spent many hours travelling around Berlin by tram and S-Bahn, visiting Jewish children hidden in secret locations, taking them food, money and forged papers. She became concerned that Jewish children were missing out on their education because they were in hiding or barred from school, so started to tutor some in her home.

The circle around Elisabeth Abegg protected three Jewish children under the age of 14. Hildegard Knies, who specialized in child nurture, took particular care of these youngsters, teaching them to use assumed names and inventing false life stories for them. Such children could not be allowed to speak openly for fear of giving themselves away, and had to learn to adjust quickly to living with different host families and to hiding their fears and anxieties. They had to pretend they had suffered various illnesses to conceal the fact that they had never attended school, having been prevented by the Nazis. These children also had to affect to follow the religion of whoever was hiding them – whether Lutheran or Catholic – and if necessary attend Christian services. The younger the children, the more intensely Knies had to monitor their behaviour. Some adapted easily to role play and adopting fictitious life stories, but others desperately wanted to talk about their 'real' life. After the war, Hildegard Knies became concerned about the psychological trauma such children suffered as a result of these experiences.

Knies and her aunt Christine Engler tried to protect Herta and Ernst Goldstein and their four-year-old daughter, Evelyn ('Evi'), who went underground in March 1943 after evading the 'Factory Action'. The family initially hid in Engler's grocery shop, but then had to split up. Hildegard Knies took in

Evi and had to teach the lively little girl not to tell strangers her real name, not to talk about her Jewish pre-school and never to say anything about her family. Several times they had to find a new hiding place after she inadvertently revealed too much. On one occasion Evi started to pray in Hebrew at a Lutheran kindergarten, so had to be moved quickly. In late June 1943 helpers found a safe lodging for Evi in Bloestau (now Vishnev-ka, Russia), east of Königsberg, East Prussia, in the country house of the Bunke family, where she remained safe until the end of the war. Meanwhile, Evi's father Ernst was caught in a Gestapo trap and in August 1943 deported to Auschwitz, where he was murdered. Following Ernst's arrest, his wife Herta was concealed by Hildegard Knies and Richard Linde among others, and in February 1944 joined her daughter Evi at the Bunkes' home in Bloestau.

Abegg's friends also helped Ludwig Collm (1901–77), a bap-tized secondary-school teacher who had been dismissed in 1933 because of his Jewish roots. When his family was ordered to report for deportation, he fled his flat with his wife, Steffi, and six-year-old daughter, Susanne ('Susi'). 'The transport was designated for Poland,' he explained. 'The meaning of this we knew all too well. After long discussion we decided to . . . try to rescue our lives . . . On 12 December [1942] we locked up our apartment facing an incalculable fate.' A Social Democrat put Collm in touch with Elisabeth Abegg:

> With a beating heart I rang the bell . . . But I relaxed when a white-haired lady with benign, well-balanced features opened the door and immediately let me in. I didn't have to tell her much about our suffering: she was already

well-informed and knew of the problems of the 'submarines'. She said at once warmly she would help us in any way . . . Within days she found me lodgings with a working-class family at the Silesian Railway Station . . . My wife's first meeting with Elisabeth Abegg was unforgettable. They met at the Lietzenburger Strasse post office using a pre-arranged signal. With tears in her eyes my wife thanked her for her help. Dr Abegg demurred, saying: 'We are in your debt! We have so much to atone for!'

The couple stayed briefly with Hildegard Knies, while Susi spent several months sheltering with Bertha Becker in Lindow. The three family members each hid separately in a number of different places until finally reunited on 7 February 1944, at 'Haus Felicitas', Horst-Seebad, Pomerania (today Niechorze, Poland), on the Baltic coast, where Ludwig was able to use forged documents to claim he was a bombed-out civil servant and work as a tutor. The Collms were still safe in Pomerania when it was liberated.

After the war, Ludwig Collm drew up a list of the different places where he, his wife Steffi and daughter Susi had stayed between December 1942 and February 1944:[11]

Ludwig

| Löffke | 10 days |
| Blumenthal | 1 day |

---

11 *Die Juden in Deutschland 1933–1945*, ed. Wolfgang Benz, C. H. Beck, Munich, 1988.

Grünbaum	2 days
Bielke	20 days
Seleu, Teltow	14 days
Fischer, Teltow	6 months
Sachisthal	2 months
Meta	2 months
Kleingarn	8 days
Oranienburg	September 1943 – 7 February 1944[12]

Steffi

Meise	10 days
Löffke	
Sachisthal	
Kny	
Rooms in Neukölln	1 April 1943 – 7 February 1944

Susi

Meise	10 days
Kny	3 weeks
Meta	3 weeks
Lewin	2 weeks
Frankenberg	4 weeks
Gräser	4 months
Mucha	4 months
With Bertha Becker in Lindow	6 months

---

12 Oranienburg was the site of an early concentration camp, replaced by Sachsenhausen concentration camp in 1936.

Dr Abegg and her circle also helped the Neumann family. Rita Neumann, her younger brother, Ralph, and their widowed mother, Gertrud, were conscripted for forced labour in Berlin. In February 1943, they went into hiding to avoid deportation, but after just a few weeks Gertrud was arrested and died in police custody. Helped by her daughters, Ruth and Angelika, Agnes Wendland (1891–1946), director of women's aid and wife of one of the pastors at the leading Confessing Church, Gethsemanekirche at Prenzlauer Berg in northeast Berlin, was harbouring Jewish 'U-boats' in their flat in Gethsemanestrasse without her husband Walter's knowledge. 'Rita stayed at our house,' Wendland's daughter, Angelika, recalled. 'She helped in the house . . . One day Rita was crying a lot. When mother asked why, she said her brother [aged only sixteen] was riding the S-Bahn all day and spending the night in public toilets. Mother said he could come and live with us too. They both hid in the parsonage for almost two years.'

To avoid attracting suspicion, Ralph had to pretend he had a job, so he started to spend his day at Elisabeth Abegg's flat, where she tutored him a little – as a Jew, he had been prevented from completing his schooling. Abegg obtained ID papers for Rita, registering her as her niece, and explaining to officials that she had come from another city but lost her documents in an air raid. In February 1945 Ralph Neumann was arrested during a railway station ID check, following which the Gestapo beat him so badly at their Oranienstrasse HQ that he divulged Frau Wendland's name. The Gestapo then arrested her and sent her to the prison camp at Grosse Hamburger Strasse 26, Berlin, for three weeks. When she became ill, they agreed that her daughter Ruth could stand in for her. Ralph's sister Rita was also arrested. The night before the two siblings were due to be deported, they managed to escape from the third floor of Schulstrasse prison, Wedding, by sliding down a washing line. They were now harboured in the homes of a prison chaplain named Pastor Harald Poelchau (1903–72)[13] and of Dr Seitz, who belonged to an underground group known as 'Uncle Emil'. The Neumanns survived the war and emigrated to the USA in 1946.[14]

The people Dr Abegg hid in her flat had mostly to stay indoors, even during air raids. Occasionally her sister Julie took them to the local air-raid shelter, where they had to sit among Nazis. A trained seamstress, Julie Abegg mended and altered clothing for those in hiding, and obtained hair dye to help change their appearance. On long train journeys to a new hiding place some of the Jewish women dressed as widows, hoping this might discourage thorough inspection by officials.

Every Friday Jewish fugitives and others persecuted by the Nazis came for lunch at Elisabeth's flat. 'You gave us far more than bodily food,' Liselotte recalled later. 'For two hours we could talk about the world of art and science and forget we could no longer live like human beings.' A guest named Schäfer said, 'I couldn't have stood my time underground without the Friday lunches at the Abegg sisters' flat.'

---

13 Poelchau belonged to the circle around von Moltke that made an unsuccessful coup attempt on 20 July 1944.

14 *Memories from My Early Life in Germany 1926–1946*, by Ralph Neumann, 2006, is available as a free download on the website of the *Gedenkstätte Deutscher Widerstand*/German Resistance Memorial Center, Berlin.

Dr Elisabeth Abegg, Berlin

Ralph Neumann's twentieth birthday, 22 May 1946, at Wannsee,
Berlin. Ralph Neumann is centre back; Elisabeth Abegg far
right; Ruth Wendland second from right and her sister Angelika
Rutenborn, née Wendland, second from left

Copyright private owner; scan German Resistance Memorial Museum, Berlin

On one occasion Dr Abegg's briefcase was stolen on the S-Bahn: it contained ration cards for fugitives, the transcript of a speech by the anti-Nazi émigré author Thomas Mann and Elisabeth's ID card. The police arrested the thief, but fortunately he had mixed up things he had stolen from a number of different people, so it was unclear who owned the incriminating items.

Quakers believe in speaking the truth; yet Elisabeth Abegg lied to the Gestapo, her neighbours and anyone else who needed to be kept in the dark. She offered not only safety, protection and food but also kindness, reassurance and goodness. Dr Abegg told a friend that one of the evils perpetrated by the Nazis was making everyone notice what made other people different: seeing this person as Jewish, this one as German and so forth. Constantly exposed to Nazi propaganda, even people who hated Nazism apparently couldn't prevent themselves from noting such distinctions.

A Jewish woman named Charlotte Herzfeld, rescued by Abegg after her parents committed suicide, said years later, 'You were there – calm, serene, courageous . . . I regained trust, I sensed warmth, I felt safe. You reminded me of my mother's calmness, warmth and equanimity.' 'She encouraged us not to despair and to believe in a better future,' agreed Yitzhak Schwersenz. 'I always think of her [Abegg] as a guardian angel in the midst of that terrible hell. She acted, not for compensation, but out of love for the persecuted.'

Dr Abegg witnessed that she accommodated 12 people in her flat – mainly Jews, but also people facing political persecution, such as the social-democratic resistance fighter Ernst von Harnack (1888–1945), in hiding after the failed assassination attempt on Hitler in the summer of 1944.[15] All told, Elisabeth Abegg and her friends helped far more: it is estimated that through their network around 80 people were given lodging and supported with food, money, clothing and forged documents. Most survived. Miraculously, Dr Abegg's activities were never discovered or denounced.

After the war, relationships between helpers and those saved often became difficult. Many lost contact with each other in the chaotic post-war circumstances, and some of those who had been saved felt burdened by feeling they owed their life to their rescuers and sometimes avoided any contact. Others developed lifelong friendships with their helpers, and even some survivors who emigrated maintained contact and returned to Germany for visits.

After the war Abegg returned to teaching, sharing her flat with another Quaker, Katharina Provinzki (1905–95). By now, 'white-haired and angelic', she was acting as clerk of the Berlin Quaker meeting.[16] Liselotte Pereles became a Berlin social worker and remained close to Elisabeth Abegg – 'always calm and kindly, always only thinking of our welfare and our safety, fearless for herself'. Dr Abegg eventually adopted Pereles as her daughter.

On her seventy-fifth birthday in 1957, some survivors dedicated a collection of memoirs to Dr Abegg, entitled *When One*

---

15 Von Harnack was executed on 5 March 1945 for his part in the abortive uprising.

16 Other leading members included the Halle and Hoffman families, Martha Rohn ('a dear old lady'), and a leading Young Quaker named Thea Horleborg. Hugh W. Maw, *The Training and Experiences of a Quaker Relief Worker 1946–48*, Words by Design, Oxfordshire, 2014, p. 138.

The apartment block at Tempelhofer Damm, Dr Abegg's former home.
The memorial plaque can be seen on the left of the entrance

Copyright © Silent Heroes Memorial Center, Berlin

Light Pierced the Darkness. It contained a number of moving testimonies, including this one by Hertha Blumenthal:

> With Fräulein Dr. Abegg was revealed the truth that a life of love for one's fellow human beings, together with respect for others, is the most elevated and eternal value . . . Her rectitude, straightforwardness and endless love will always be the model . . . upon which I pattern my life and will come into play whenever anyone needs my help.

Jizchak Schwersenz summed up the contribution of Dr Elisabeth Abegg and her helpers in this way: 'Through their Christian faith, conviction and humanity the people who stood by us were strong enough to face fear. They realized what was happening when their neighbours were driven off on trucks and their belongings were dragged away . . .'

On 3 March 1957 Dr Abegg received the Order of Merit of the Federal Republic of Germany; ten years later on 23 May 1967 she was recognized as one of the Righteous Among the Nations, as were later Hildegard Arnold-Knies, Frieda and Adolf Bunke, Margrit Dobbeck, Bertha Gerhardt, Elisabeth Schmitz, Agnes and Ruth Wendland and Lydia Forsström.

Dr Abegg died on 8 August 1974 aged 92. On 9 November 1991 a memorial plaque was placed at Tempelhofer Damm 56, her former home, in the presence of Jizchak Schwersenz and Hildegard Arnold, née Knies. In 2006 a street in Berlin's Mitte district was named after her, as was a Protestant primary school in Berlin-Prenzlauer Berg.

6

The constant midwife

STANISŁAWA LESZCZYŃSKA, ŁÓDŹ

Stanisława Leszczyńska, a Polish midwife, was sent to Auschwitz for aiding Jews in the Łódź ghetto. At the death camp she delivered more than 3,000 babies in the filthy 'hospital', disobeying strict orders to slaughter them all at birth.

Stanisława Zambrzycki was born in Baluty, a poor area of Łódź, on 8 May 1896 to a Polish carpenter named Jan and his wife, Henryka. Her father was drafted into the army and her mother worked 12-hour shifts at the huge Poznański textile factory to enable Stanisława to attend school. In 1916 Stanisława married a printer named Bronisław Leszczyński; they had four children. Qualifying as a midwife in 1922, Stanisława worked in poorer areas of Łódź. Since babies were usually delivered at home, she had to be available at any time of day and sometimes walked miles to the homes of expectant women.

In September 1939 Germany invaded Poland. As early as 8 September German troops occupied the city of Łódź, which they renamed Litzmannstadt. The population of Łódź numbered 672,000, of whom one-third – 230,000 – were Jewish. In a secret order of 10 December 1939 the German governor

Stanisława Leszczyńska

of the city ordered the creation of the first large Jewish ghetto: 'only a transitional arrangement . . . the ultimate objective must be completely to burn out this plague spot'. By May 1940 the ghetto was closed off: after this date any Jew found outside it without authorization was liable to be shot. As a result 164,000 Jews were penned into an area of just 1.5 square miles and forced to work for the Nazis. On 1 October 1940 the Germans declared Łódź city centre *Judenrein* – cleansed of Jews.

Because their house stood inside the ghetto limits, the Roman Catholic Leszczyńska family were forced to move from their home in Żurawia Street to Wspólna 3 Street. Horrified by what they heard of conditions in the ghetto, Stanisława Leszczyńska and her family – including all four children – joined the efforts of the growing Polish resistance movement and started to help the Jews by taking food and fake ID documents into the ghetto.

Denounced by an informer, on 18 February 1943 Stanisława and her three younger children, Sylwia, Stanisław and Henryk, were arrested by the Gestapo in the act of assisting the Jews. Her husband had been creating false IDs and other documents at his print shop and with their oldest son was actively involved in the resistance. Both managed to avoid arrest and fled the city. Stanisława was now separated from her two younger sons, who were sent as slave labourers to the stone quarries of Mauthausen-Gusen concentration camp in Austria. Her husband Bronisław died in the Warsaw Uprising of 1944; she never saw him again.

After interrogation by the Gestapo, Stanisława and her 24-year-old daughter Sylwia were transported to Oświęcim (Auschwitz-Birkenau) concentration camp on 17 April 1943, tattooed with the numbers 41335 and 41336 respectively and confined in a non-Jewish section of the camp. Both women had their heads shaved, were stripped of their belongings and given basic camp clothing: coarse underwear and striped overalls, all infested with lice. Sylwia was allotted two left-foot

Łódź (Litzmannstadt) ghetto, Poland

Wiki commons PD

slippers. Despite searches by camp guards, Leszczyńska somehow managed to retain her midwifery certificate.

Auschwitz comprised a variety of buildings, including overcrowded sleeping quarters, offices, kitchens and latrines. It also had five 'infirmary' blocks where, in appalling conditions, sick prisoners were looked after mainly by doctors who were themselves prisoners. The German doctors were afraid of contracting infections, so used medically trained prisoners to work in the camp hospitals. Anyone reckoned unlikely to recover from their illness was killed. To allow people who otherwise would have been eliminated to remain on the ward, prisoner-doctors often concealed serious cases by falsifying the records. Many Auschwitz prisoners suffered from dysentery, typhoid and typhus, for which the Nazi authorities would send them to be liquidated. Thanks to the prisoner-doctors, such diseases frequently went unreported or were misreported as 'flu'.

Soon after she arrived, Stanisława contracted typhus and was taken to the 'hospital'. As she was recovering, she heard that a German nurse had lost her job in the camp. She decided to try to replace her and showed a camp doctor her midwife's certificate. When she also demonstrated she had a good command of German, she was ordered to help pregnant women prisoners and assist with the delivery of their babies.

Stanisława spent the next two years serving as a midwife in Block 20, the women's 'medical facility', which consisted of a 40-metre-/130-foot-long wooden barrack room. Lining the two longer walls were filthy three-layered bunks, on each of which three or four women had to sleep. The straw mattresses were worn stiff and alive with vermin. The camp was situated in a low-lying area, so the barracks frequently flooded to a depth of several inches of water. Between 1,000 and 1,200 patients occupied this sick ward, of whom at least a dozen died every day. 'In winter, when the temperatures were very low, icicles formed on the ceiling from breath and perspiration,' Stanisława recalled years later. 'Beneath these icicles, people slept and sick women delivered their babies.' The block was overwhelmed by infections such as dysentery and typhoid. Rats were everywhere, their victims sick women and newborn babies. An appalling stench filled the room.

The women came mainly from Poland, Ukraine, Greece and Yugoslavia. The only place in any way suitable for deliveries was a brick stove in the centre of the room that was lit just a few times a year. The 30 bunks nearest to it constituted the 'maternity ward'. 'The fate of women in labour was tragic and the role of the midwife extremely difficult,' Stanisława reported afterwards. 'There were no antiseptics, no dressings and no medicine apart from a small ration of aspirin.' Food consisted mainly of rotten boiled greens and hard bread.

On arrival at Auschwitz, most pregnant women were sent directly to the gas chambers. Heinrich Himmler had ordered that 'women and children had to be killed to eliminate "the germ cell of a new Jewish revival"'.[1] Women who discovered they were pregnant at the camp were sometimes given an abortion by a Romanian gynaecologist named Gisella Perl (1907–88), a Jewish prisoner selected by Josef Mengele to

---

1   Phyllis Lester and Danny M. Cohen, Introduction to Gisella Perl, *I Was a Doctor in Auschwitz*, Lexington Books, London, 2019, p. 16.

administer a hospital ward in the death camp.[2] Without proper equipment, medication or beds, she worked to comfort the starving, diseased and dying. She soon realized that the Germans were deceiving women as they arrived when they asked if they were pregnant. They promised pregnant women they would be sent to a camp with better living conditions and double bread rations, but in fact brutalized them before dispatching them to the gas chambers. Many were summarily executed. A minority managed to conceal their pregnancy, knowing that both they and their infant would be killed if they were found to be pregnant. Such women often gave birth secretly in their dormitory. The rest were sent to the 'medical facility' to complete their pregnancy in the squalid conditions described above.

A midwife known as 'Sister Klara', sent to Auschwitz as punishment for child murder, oversaw the 'maternity ward' along with a redhead known as 'Sister Pfani', previously a prostitute. Klara told Stanisława that every child delivered had to be 'disposed of' and registered as 'stillborn'. Stanisława's son Bronisław claimed Klara 'beat [his] mother on the head . . . for not obeying her instructions . . . She was then called to the *Lagerarzt* [camp doctor] who ordered her to perform infanticide if she wanted to survive. He was surprised when this small, weak woman, who he could crush with his boot, replied: "No, never."' Bronisław added, 'Why they did not kill her then, no one knows.'

---

2 Lester and Cohen describe as a 'choiceless choice' the performance of abortion and infanticide to save the lives of women who would otherwise have been sent to be gassed along with their infants and foetuses. Perl, *I Was a Doctor in Auschwitz*.

Each newborn baby was supposed to be drowned in a water barrel within full sight and hearing of its mother, and then registered as 'stillborn'. Guilty of *Berufsverbrecherin* (occupational crime), Klara was, under German regulations, barred from practising her profession, so did not assist with the actual delivery of the babies. The historian Michael Berkowitz notes this grotesque example of the Nazis' 'on the one hand, cynically adhering to "legal" standards – not allowing a disbarred nurse to assist with deliveries – but on the other hand, assigning her to murder new-born Jewish babies'.

Stanisława refused to drown the newborns – and continued to refuse despite repeated orders. She apparently even stood up to Dr Josef Mengele, the camp's infamous 'Angel of Death', known for his brutal experiments on twins and other inmates.[3] According to her son, speaking in 1988, Stanisława told Mengele that these babies ought not to be killed, to which he responded furiously: '*Befehl ist befehl*' ('Orders are orders!').

Leszczyńska reckoned she delivered some 3,000 babies during the two years between April 1943 and the liberation of Auschwitz in spring 1945. At first she had to manage on her own, with occasional help from her daughter. 'The German camp physicians – Rhode, Koenig and Mengele – would not, of course, soil their medical vocations by helping non-Germans.' Later, Stanisława was assisted by women prisoners who were doctors.

Stanisława Leszczyńska delivered the babies as professionally as she could, despite the threats and beatings of *Schwester* Klara. The pregnant mothers apparently didn't realize their

---

3   Dr Perl reported that Mengele became 'excited' when twins were delivered.

The entrance to Block 10 at Auschwitz, where Josef Mengele and other German doctors used male and female prisoners in live experiments

Wiki commons

infants had little or no life expectancy, and many bartered their inadequate rations for scraps of fabric to use as nappies after their baby was born. There was no running water in the 'ward': any water had to be carried in a bucket for a considerable distance. There were no drugs or painkillers, few blankets, a single pair of scissors and minimal food. A baby's umbilical cord had to be knotted with a scrap of cloth. Stanisława took particular care to wash healthy infants before bathing the sick babies so as to avoid infecting yet more infants – all the while fully aware that almost every baby she delivered would shortly be killed.

Not quite every baby was murdered. Some Gentile women were allowed to keep their babies, though they usually perished in the appalling conditions of the camp. A minuscule number of Jewish babies were allowed to live, though it is unclear what happened to them. After 1943, a few infants were allotted to German families as so-called 'Aryan' babies under Nazi Germany's *Lebensborn* programme, which abducted up to 100,000 children from Poland alone.[4] Non-Jewish children with such Aryan characteristics as blue eyes and blond hair were sent to the town of Nakła (Naklo) to be 'de-nationalized' before being dispatched to orphanages or placed with German parents. Leszczyńska said she attempted to tattoo such babies under the armpit before they were removed in the probably vain hope they might later be identified and reunited with their mothers, though there is no corroborative evidence for this.

---

4 For an account of the *Lebensborn* 'experiment', see Catrine Clay and Michael Leapman, *Master Race: The Lebensborn experiment in Nazi Germany*, Hodder & Stoughton, London, 1995.

Some mothers killed their own babies rather than hand them over to the Nazis.

Stanisława Leszczyńska said later that she felt completely helpless as she watched the babies she had delivered being murdered or starved to death as their mothers were prevented from breastfeeding them. No extra food or milk was allocated

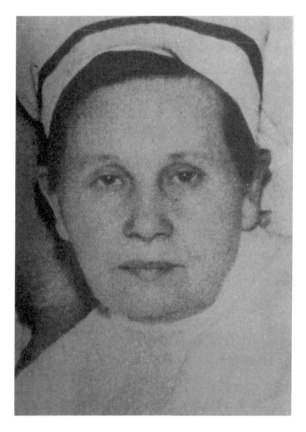

Stanisława Leszczyńska in her midwife's uniform

for infants, who died agonizingly slowly from malnutrition. This Polish midwife continued working tirelessly day and night, lavishing love on babies she knew would mostly live so very briefly.

Stanisława baptized children with a given name if the mother was Christian and requested it. She was deeply religious and prayed for problem-free labour and delivery. According to Maria Saloman, a camp survivor, 'Before making a delivery, [Stanisława] made the sign of the cross and prayed. She whispered a prayer in which she . . . asked for help and hope . . . She worked only for us, day after day, night after night.' Some of the women called her 'Mother' for her love. Stanisława claimed that no mother or baby died under her care.

Saloman's memories continue:

For weeks she never had a chance to lie down. Sometimes she sat down near a patient on the stove, dozed for a moment, but soon jumped up and ran to one of the moaning women . . . My baby managed to last three months in the camp, but seemed doomed to die of starvation. I was completely devoid of milk. 'Mother' somehow found two women – an Estonian and a Russian – to wet-nurse my baby. To this day I do not know at what price. My Liz owes her life to Stanisława Leszczynska. I cannot think of her without tears coming to my eyes.

Stanisława's son, who later practised as a doctor, wrote, 'One woman told me that for two days and two nights my mother helped her to give birth. She recalled how my mother wove her plaits as she helped her through her pain.'

On one occasion Leszczyńska was assisting a woman from Vilnius who had been found guilty of helping the partisans. She recalled:

Immediately after she gave birth they called her [prisoner] number. I went to explain why she was absent, but that only made them angrier. I knew they were summoning her to the crematorium. She wrapped the baby in dirty paper and pressed it to her breast. Her lips moved silently; it seemed she wanted to sing a song to her little one, as mothers sometimes did, humming different lullabies, trying to compensate for the cold, the hunger and the misery. But she didn't have enough strength to make her voice heard; only tears fell on her baby's head.

A prisoner-doctor named Elzbieta Pawlowska remembered Stanisława leading prayers in the barrack room:

We would sit on the bunks. 'Mother' would start a prayer and then we would sing. We sang quietly. It was not possible otherwise. It was only a moment – between fifteen and thirty minutes – but it was very peaceful. She was able to create a special atmosphere. Russian women from nearby wards came to participate.

Corrie ten Boom did something similar at Ravensbrück.[5]

---

5 See p. 119.

Years later, in her book *The Report of a Midwife from Auschwitz*,[6] Stanisława described how she risked her life to save the newborns. In the camp there were on average four births every day. Of the 3,000 babies she is believed to have delivered, medical historians Susan Benedict and Linda Shields reckon 1,500 were drowned by nurses Klara and Pfani; a further 1,000 died of cold and starvation, deliberately deprived of their mother's milk; and about 500 were stolen for the *Lebensborn* programme. Only about 30 survived with their mothers in the camp.

Stanisława continued as midwife for the duration of the war, until Auschwitz was liberated on 26 January 1945. The Nazis forced most Auschwitz inmates to depart on a 'death march' to another camp. Leszczyńska refused to leave because many sick prisoners couldn't walk. Leokadia Niewiadomska, another inmate, recalled:

Between 18 and 19 January 1945 an SS man came to the maternity block and ordered everyone to prepare for the evacuation. Mrs Leszczyńska quickly baptized several children. The women were on their last legs, among them many mothers with tiny children. They stood waiting in the cold for hours, just in shirts, with thin black blankets thrown over their shoulders . . . It was a terrible night. The very sick and feeding mothers knew they had to stay . . . Ms. Leszczyńska, her daughter and Dr. Konieczna stayed with us. Without hesitating, they

---

6   *Raport położnej z Oświęcimia*, 1965.

turned down the chance to escape and remained . . . until the end.

Stanisława waited until the Red Cross arrived and the camp was fully liberated, not leaving until 2 February.

After the war Stanisława Leszczyńska returned to Łódź and continued to work as a midwife until her retirement in 1958. Only then did she reveal some of her wartime experiences. Her work lived on in the memories of survivors whose babies she had attempted to give a dignified birth, and in the lives of the tiny minority of children who survived and left the camp alive. When Kazimera Bogdanska was unable to nurse her tiny daughter, Stanisława told her that she should give the child her empty breast 'so the glands wouldn't stop working'. Bogdanska confirmed years later that:

> Mother was right. How lucky that I believed her. When liberty came in January 1945, and I was taken to a proper hospital with typhoid fever, the doctor let me continue giving my child my milk-less breast. After a time, the milk returned. My daughter began to gain weight . . . She started to grow round and rosy-cheeked . . . Mother's wisdom and faith saved my only child.

Twenty-five years later, on 27 January 1970, Stanisława attended a commemoration in Warsaw where she met some of the women whose children had been born at Auschwitz, and the newly composed *Oratorium Oświęcimskie* (Auschwitz Oratorio) by Alina Nowak was performed at the Grand Theatre.

Stanisława Leszczyńska died on 11 March 1974. In 1983 the Kraków School of Obstetricians was named after her, as was a road at Auschwitz museum and a street in Łódź. In 1992 a beatification process was initiated for her.

7

The monk on a bicycle

DOM BRUNO REYNDERS, BRUSSELS

Henri Reynders – an intellectual and self-confessed 'anarchist' monk – spent much of the Second World War criss-crossing parts of Belgium on his bike, sheltering and shepherding fugitive Jewish children.

Henri Reynders was born in Brussels on 24 October 1903, the fifth of eight children in a middle-class Catholic family. At the age of 17 he was accepted as a candidate for holy orders and entered the Catholic University of Louvain. In 1925 he took vows as a Benedictine monk – 'Dom Bruno' – and attached himself to the 'intellectual abbey' of Mont César (now Keizersberg) in Louvain, Belgium. He was supposed to lecture on theology but discovered he had little talent as a teacher, worrying his conservative abbot by promoting some of Martin Luther's Protestant ideas. The maverick monk was instead employed as tutor to the duc de Guise's son, a claimant to the French throne. 'Me, an anarchist, teaching a prince!' he later commented.

Dom Bruno travelled extensively within Belgium and beyond, lecturing and debating. During a 1938 visit to Germany he witnessed the 'shocking, revolting and nauseating' brutality of Nazi anti-Semitism. In 1971 he recalled the following:

> I was strolling in a busy street. Everywhere I saw insulting signs: *Jude = Juda* ['Jew = Judas']; *Juden heraus* ['Jews out!'] and *Hier sind Juden nicht erwünscht* ['Jews are not welcome here']. This greatly shocked me – but what really revolted me was an incident I witnessed. An old man arrived, bearded, dressed in a caftan and wearing an old black hat . . . He was walking stooped, not daring to raise his eyes, hiding his face with his hand. Passers-by moved away from him as if he had the plague, bullied him or pointed a finger and sneered. This really upset me, this segregation, this contempt, this arrogance, this cruel stupidity . . . It still lingers in my memory and makes me feel sick.

Following the German invasion of Poland in September 1939, Belgium mobilized for war and Bruno Reynders was appointed chaplain of the 41st Artillery Regiment. The German army rapidly overran Belgium in May 1940. During the fighting Father Bruno sustained a leg injury and spent the following six months in German prisoner-of-war camps in Wolfsburg and Doessel giving religious and moral support to his fellow prisoners.

After King Leopold of Belgium entered negotiations with Hitler, Germany released many Belgian prisoners. Dom Bruno was able to return to Mont César and continue teaching. He made contact with the Belgian Resistance and started to help with the escape of British pilots shot down over Belgium. He also began working with, but independently of, the Jewish Defence Committee – the CDJ (*Comité de Defense des Juifs*) – a clandestine organization providing shelter for Jews on the run.

In contrast with their policy during the First World War, Germany imposed a relatively lenient occupation on Belgium. Although the Belgian army laid down its arms, its government moved to London. The country retained virtual autonomy over internal matters and continued to govern according to its existing legal code. In late 1940, when Germany attempted to impose anti-Jewish measures, the Belgian government, civic authorities and educational institutions all reacted strongly, as did Cardinal van Roeg, the leader of the Catholic Church. In the sole instance in German-occupied countries, the defeated administration made strong efforts to frustrate the German anti-Semitic programme.

At the beginning of the war there were some 90,000 Jews in Belgium. When the country was initially occupied by Germany, most Belgian Jews fled to France, but by the summer of 1940 around half had returned. As the Final Solution was set in motion in spring 1942, around 60,000 Jews remained in Belgium, of whom about half were deported to death camps in the east.

Cardinal van Roeg encouraged his clergy to find shelter in particular for Jewish children, making it clear there should be no pressure for them to convert to Catholicism. The Bishop of Liège, Monsignor Louis-Joseph Kerkhofs (1878–1962), was particularly active in urging his clergy to rescue and protect fugitive Jews, and in 1981 was recognized as one of Yad Vashem's Righteous Among the Nations. Joseph Lepkifker, Grand Rabbi of Liège, was concealed at Banneu Monastery under the pseudonym M. l'Abbé Boty, while his wife Tzivica was hidden at a convent at Huy, and later in the little convent of *Les Soeurs du Bon Secours* in Liège.

Meanwhile Dom Bruno was dispatched to the hamlet of Hodbomont to act as chaplain to a small Catholic home for the blind. He had not been there long before he realized the director of the home, Walter Bieser, was not blind – nor were several of its other residents, such as the Ashkenazys, an elderly couple from Vienna, or a man called Silbermann. The managers of the home and most of its residents – who did include five or six blind children – were Jews in hiding, brought there by a group of Christians opposed to Nazi policies. The children had recently been transferred from *L'Hospitalité*, a Catholic charity providing holiday camps for disadvantaged children headed by a prominent Liège lawyer named Albert Van den Berg (1890–1945). Their parents had been deported following a Gestapo raid, and Father Bruno now took them under his care.

Van den Berg and Dom Bruno started to collaborate closely. Towards the end of 1942 they recognized that it was no longer safe to house these Jewish children at Hodbomont. The villagers knew what was going on and one careless word could have resulted in disaster. The home was closed and its occupants dispersed to several different locations.

Dom Bruno now returned to his abbey at Mont César and dedicated himself to finding places of refuge for Jews. In January 1943 he managed to locate ten different Belgian families who were willing to shelter Jews, some already with several children of their own. These families included the Bodarts, Bertrands and Martens of Louvain, and others in

Jodoigne, Ciney, Brussels, Namur and Bouge. Placing Jews in these families called for much hard work, ingenuity and travel. Everything had to be improvised: food, clothing, false ID papers, false 'Aryanized' names and finances. A fellow monk provided Bruno with skilfully forged ID cards, baptismal certificates and food coupons, while Van den Berg paid for many of the necessities since Bruno, a penniless monk, owned nothing and relied completely on donations.

Dom Bruno began to find support in a number of different places, including his fellow monks at Mont César, the hierarchy of the Belgian Catholic Church and his own family. His teenage nephew Michel sometimes acted as a courier, taking messages to others in the clandestine group, and escorted fugitives on short trips across Brussels. Meanwhile, the intrepid monk gradually built up an underground network, making contact with pre-existing resistance groups and individuals engaged in similar rescue work. The work was extremely dangerous, since the Nazis were actively hunting down Jews, and many Belgians were informing on and denouncing their fellow countrymen. A number of resistance workers paid with their lives.

Dom Bruno's work consisted largely of locating families and institutions willing to hide Jews. He visited Catholic institutions such as boarding schools, usually within convents and monasteries, and private families, asking them to take in Jewish children. Dom Bruno then accompanied the children to their new homes, from time to time moving them to a new location to avoid arousing suspicion among neighbours. Dom Bruno's brother's house in Ixelles, central Brussels, became a kind of transit hub for transient fugitives. During April 1943

Dom Bruno with some of the children he rescued during the Second World War

Archives of the Monastery Amay-Chevetogne

Father Bruno found shelter for 16 Jewish children and adults; in May for 17 more; and in July hiding places for 18 more.

Father Bruno also returned regularly to visit the children he had placed in homes, bringing news of their parents if they too were in hiding. At first he worked alone, receiving financial support from only Mr Van den Berg; later he also gained the support of a banker named Jules Dubois-Pelerin. As he built up his contacts with other resistance groups, Dom Bruno too had constantly to move from place to place to avoid being caught by the Gestapo.

In his journal Father Bruno talks of Bernard Rotmil, one of the boys he helped conceal:

> I recall Bernard's appetite as a sixteen-year-old boy, and the difficulty I had with this, as I paid for his upkeep at the place where he stayed in Louvain. One day I ventured to tell him to try and control his appetite. I recall his distraught face as he replied, 'But I'm always hungry!' I was completely disarmed and didn't stop reproaching myself for intervening. But at that time food was difficult to find and expensive.

In due course Bernard was placed on a farm where food was plentiful and where he remained safely till the end of the war.

In his memoirs, Father Bruno also described how he recruited Professor Luyckx from the University of Louvain as a helper. Having described the problem and his need for help, the priest awaited a response from the academic. After an awkward silence, the priest said, 'Professor, can I ask what your answer is?'

'But, Father, I was awaiting yours,' replied Luyckx. 'You told me things of which I was unaware. I should probably have known about them, but I was in all honesty ignorant. Why did you come to see me? Because you know I am a Christian. You pointed out my duty as a Christian. So my answer is: When are you bringing me a Jewish child?'

The Gestapo eventually got wind of Father Bruno's activities and on 4 January 1944 raided his office at Mont César Abbey when he was involved in his 159th rescue. In the nick of time he managed to hide incriminating documents, including lists of the false names under which children were being concealed. After this raid, and urged by his Superior, Father Bruno went into hiding. He exchanged his monk's habit for civilian clothing and took to wearing a beret to hide his monk's tonsure. But regardless of the danger he continued his rescue work, basing himself first in Louvain and then in Brussels – next door to the office of an SS captain in the Office of Jewish Affairs. From this address Father Bruno organized a further 150 rescues, hiding Jews even at this dangerous location before transferring them to a safer refuge.

Supported by Bishop Kerkhofs of Liège and Albert Van den Berg, Father Bruno placed children in a number of different Catholic institutions, including the Sisters of Bellegem, the House of Leffe, the Benedictine Abbey of Liège, St Mary's boarding house at La Bouverie, the Jolimont Clinic, the nuns of Don Bosco in Courtrai [Kortrijk] and elsewhere. Meanwhile, Albert Van den Berg placed Jewish children in three Capuchin Banneux monastic houses, where Father Jamin and monks named Avelin, Fulbert and Jaminet looked after them.

In April 1943 Albert Van den Berg was arrested. Initially given a light sentence, after release he was re-arrested by the Gestapo and sent to the Neuengamme concentration camp, near Hamburg, Germany. He survived until the end of the war, but died of exhaustion before he could return home to Belgium. In 1995 Van den Berg was recognized as one of the Righteous Among the Nations.

Despite several close calls, Dom Bruno continued his dangerous mission for the rest of the German occupation. He kept detailed records – fortunately never discovered by the Nazis – containing the names of more than 350 men, women and children whom he tried to help, together with important details of his rescue work.

In later years many of those he concealed and saved expressed their appreciation. One of them, named Gilles Rozberg, recalled:

> One night in 1943, just after I had turned thirteen, I met Father Bruno on the street. He didn't know me, but I recognized him by the way he walked, the cloak he wore and his elegant tall hat. I threw myself at him and asked him to help me. After a few moments' suspicion and concern, he said he was prepared to help. Two weeks later, my younger brother and I were taken to a hiding place.

Flora Singer-Mendalavitz recounted a similar story:

> I don't know exactly how I first made contact with Dom Bruno . . . Dom Bruno found a new hiding place for us and gave my mother instructions on how to get to the

northern railway station with her three children. There we would meet a woman waiting for us dressed in a particular way. According to the instructions, we had to follow this woman into her carriage on the train without kissing our mother or even saying goodbye. We did as we were told, and after the train pulled out of the station, the woman turned to us, kissed us and told us we were being taken to a safe place. After the Liberation, we went to live in Brussels and Dom Bruno visited us regularly. He helped us and brought us food. He always asked my mother if she needed anything. Dom Bruno registered me in a Catholic school and for courses in typing, painting and piano, taught by one of the sisters in the convent. Dom Bruno paid for everything. Even today . . . I see Dom Bruno's face in front of me and say 'Thank you.' When he registered me for the Catholic school, he gave strict orders to exempt me from Christian worship and religious instruction classes.

Rachelle Goldstein was only three years old and living in Brussels when early in 1943 her parents contacted Father Bruno: 'He came to our house and I was just told I was being taken to the country for an outing.' Bruno took Rachelle and two young cousins to Bruges by train. When they were stopped by German soldiers, Father Bruno talked his way out of danger. He took the children to a Dominican convent that had a nursery. Rachelle burst into tears when she realized she would be staying there. A few months later a resistance worker visited and brought a doll from her mother: 'She told me my parents knew where I was,' she recalled later. 'That meant everything to me.'

Jack Goldstein was nine when in 1944 his mother took him with his twin brother to meet Father Bruno at another railway station. The priest gave them new names and ID papers and took them to stay the night with a doctor, who next day drove them to their hiding place, concealed under a blanket in the back of his car. The doctor and Father Bruno talked their way through several German roadblocks to reach the convent where the twins were to spend the next six months. 'I didn't know if I would ever see my parents again,' said Mr Goldstein. 'I lived in fear. I studied Christianity. I went to church every morning, but I knew my Jewish heritage.'

Fifty years later, Jack Goldstein recalled the Belgian priest fondly: 'He saw what was being done was wrong . . . I don't know how many people would have done what he did. Père Bruno . . . was a slender, gentle man in his thirties, with sharp eyes twinkling out from behind the spectacles of a scholar.' 'Père Bruno always found time to visit us every week, to make sure we were well treated,' remembered another Jewish child, Zvika Arlav. 'He would appear without warning – day or night, rain, sun or snow: we always felt we were under his protective wings.' Another survivor, Esther Krygiev, remarked that Father Bruno was 'very gentle, very fatherly . . . He would take us by the hand and explain that where we were going we shouldn't say we were Jewish . . . not even trust other children, but keep everything to ourselves . . . To me he represented security and trust . . . He was the only one with the gift to remove our fears.'

Just before the Germans retreated, Father Bruno made one final rescue, in the Place du Châtelain, Brussels. He found a refuge for three children who had escaped last-minute deportation and had spent the previous night in the Forest of Soignes. 'I never saw children so keen to allow themselves to be scrubbed and washed!' he recalled. He took them to the Daughters of Charity in Asse, eight miles outside Brussels, and then walked back into the capital just in time to see the German troops' final retreat.

The war had not yet finished, and Dom Bruno rejoined the Belgian armed forces as a chaplain. Before returning to his post, he visited a synagogue in Brussels:

> The rabbi stopped the service . . . The congregation gave him a tumultuous welcome. The children pressed his arms while the parents, in tears, covered him with words of thanks and blessing. It was some time before calm was restored and the service could resume in the synagogue. When I looked for Father Bruno, I couldn't see him. He had just slipped away.

After the war Flora Singer, who had been in hiding for 11 months, began to help her mother by doing paid jobs. Father Bruno asked if she would rather go to school, but her mother explained that they needed Flora's earnings to buy food. So Father Bruno started to take food to the family in order that Flora could attend school. When Flora asked why he had risked his life to save so many children, he answered, 'I just did what I'm supposed to do.' Some whom Bruno rescued called him a saint or a *tzadik* – Hebrew for a righteous man.

After the liberation, Dom Bruno helped reunite the Jewish children who had been concealed with their parents or other members of their family. Some in the Jewish community objected to attempts by a number of Christians to adopt orphaned Jewish children. A number of younger children could no longer remember their Jewish parents and wanted to stay with the Gentiles who had opened their home to them. During the occupation, Dom Bruno argued against trying to convert his charges: 'We are responsible for the lives of these children, but their souls do not belong to us,' he had declared. In most cases this principle was followed, except in a few instances of 'ignorance, excessive zeal, misguided fervour and narrow-mindedness'.

Afterwards Bruno Reynders described his policy concerning the baptism of Jewish children in Catholic homes in a carefully worded statement:

In order that the children be hidden safely they needed to live according to Christian tradition, religious practices, prayers, church attendance and religious instruction. However, many of those children who had an intellectual curiosity – uncommon among our children – and delicate and complex religious feelings, developed an enthusiasm for Catholic life and doctrine. It was impossible for believers to answer their repeated questions with . . . indifference. In the face of their sustained desire and tenacious will it was impossible and cruel to refuse baptism and conversion for two years. In almost every case baptism was conferred only with the explicit and warm approval of their parents, who were informed about the future obligations which this implied. Sometimes the parents themselves converted. The baptism of children whose parents were deported

Dom Bruno Reynders, Brussels

Dom Bruno in later life
Archives of the Monastery Amay-Chevetogne

was delayed until their parents' return where this was considered possible if not probable. The faithfulness of the children who were converted or under instruction prior to baptism is, generally speaking, noteworthy.[1]

The children for whom Father Bruno found hiding places concurred with his statements: they were consistent in later years in stating that he had instructed the convents where they were hidden not to press for conversion, but lengthy debates continued about this question.

After hostilities ceased, Father Bruno returned to his academic interests: in the 1950s he published a learned work on the Latin, Greek and Armenian vocabulary in a work by the Early Church Father Irenaeus. In 1964 Israel proclaimed Dom Bruno Reynders one of the Righteous Among the Nations and he was invited to Jerusalem to witness the planting of a tree in his honour at Yad Vashem. He responded with these words: '316 Jewish souls passed through my hands, among them 200 children. I cannot begin to tell you how many doors I knocked on. I literally wore myself out, but it was all worth it . . . Maybe Almighty God will give me a rest in the next world.'

In 1968, Dom Bruno was allowed to achieve a long-held ambition to join the ecumenically minded Chevetogne Abbey. His final post was as vicar of Ottignies, near Louvain, where he served the aged, sick and disabled. In 1975 Parkinson's disease forced him to retire to a nursing home and he died six years later, on 26 October 1981.

---

1 Dan Michman, ed., *Belgium and the Holocaust: Jews, Belgians, Germans*, Yad Vashem, Jerusalem, 1998, p. 250.

Ten years later a square in Ottignies was named in his honour, and a stele erected reading: 'Father Bruno Reynders, Benedictine (1903–1981). Hero of the Resistance. At the risk of his life saved some 400 Jews from Nazi barbarism.'

8

The Vatican Pimpernel

MONSIGNOR HUGH O'FLAHERTY, ROME

In wartime Rome three colourful but contrasting men were instrumental in facilitating the concealment and progress through enemy territory of British prisoners of war (POWs). They consisted of an Irish priest with strong republican loyalties, a titled Englishman with polished manners and expensive tastes, and a major in the Royal Artillery who twice escaped capture by the Germans: respectively Monsignor Hugh O'Flaherty, Sir Francis d'Arcy Godolphin Osborne and Major Sam Derry. Not only did this unlikely team protect and support Allied servicemen, but O'Flaherty, helped discreetly by Osborne, also concealed and protected Italian and foreign Jews in Rome.

These three cooperated in building and operating the 'Vatican Lines', or Roman escape line, through which passed some 4,000 escaping Allied POWs. Italy had joined the war on the side of the Axis powers in 1940, and many captured British servicemen were interned in camps in Italy. When Italy surrendered unconditionally to the Allies in September 1943, these British troops were given their freedom but faced the problem of getting back safely to their own lines through a country now occupied by German forces.

Hugh O'Flaherty – perhaps inevitably dubbed 'Ireland's Oskar Schindler' – was born in Lisrobin, Kiskeam, County Cork on 28 February 1898. His father was steward of the Killarney golf club and as a teenager Hugh did well at both school and golf. In 1918 he entered the Jesuit-run Mungret College, County Limerick, to train as a missionary priest. Sponsored by Bishop O'Reilly of the Archdiocese of Cape Town, in 1922 O'Flaherty went to Rome for further study and ordination. Fluent in both Italian and German, he worked as a Vatican diplomat in Egypt (1934), Haiti and Santo Domingo (1935) and Czechoslovakia (1936), before being appointed in 1938 to the staff of the Sacred Congregation of the Holy Office in Rome, previously known as the Inquisition. A six-foot-two-inch bespectacled figure, O'Flaherty combined considerable learning with a strong Irish brogue and mischievous humour.

Sir Francis d'Arcy Godolphin Osborne, 12th Duke of Leeds, had arrived in Rome in February 1936 as the new Envoy Extraordinary and Minister Plenipotentiary to the Holy See, taking up residence in the British Legation on the top floors of the Hospice of Santa Marta, just outside the Vatican. Unmarried, and with 'bubbling gaiety, simple manners, perfect courtesy and no trace of condescension', he had little money but extravagant tastes in clothes, wine, whisky and furniture.

The third in the trio, Major Sam Derry, recently escaped from German captivity, described his first meeting with Osborne in 1943, disguised as a monsignor:

Seldom have I met any man in whom I had such immediate confidence. He welcomed us warmly, yet I found it impossible to behave with anything but strict formality . . . I was almost overwhelmed by an atmosphere of old-world English courtliness and grace which I had thought belonged only to the country-house parties of long ago. Sir d'Arcy was spry, trim, a young sixty, but he had spent years enough in the diplomatic service to develop an astonishing aptitude for creating around himself an aura of all that was most civilized in English life. I felt as though I had returned home after long travels, to find that royalty had come to dinner, and I had to be on my best behaviour.

At the time of Osborne's arrival in Rome, relations between Britain and the Vatican had reached a low ebb. As an agent of a Protestant country not acting in ways approved of by the Vatican, it took some years for Osborne to gain significant influence. By the summer of 1940, however, he had become a key figure for the British in Rome.

Despite its fascist nature, Mussolini's regime did not deport any Jews from Italy. It is unclear whether *il Duce* was personally anti-Semitic: in any event, his mistress of 25 years was Jewish. Jews had played a significant role in Garibaldi's unification of Italy during the second half of the nineteenth century, after which official oppression and discrimination ended.

Yet when in the late 1930s Mussolini decided to align his regime with Hitler's Germany, one result was a new commitment to overt anti-Semitism. Italian legislation introduced in Europe's critical year of 1938 forbade marriage between Jews and Gentiles and barred Jews from serving in the armed forces. As everywhere else, there were Jew-haters among the Italian population, yet the majority were seemingly puzzled as to why their Jewish neighbours had suddenly become targets of oppression.

Even after Italy joined the war on the Axis side in 1940, persecution of Italian Jews did not increase hugely, although some foreign Jews were confined to internment camps. When in 1942, as a response to Allied landings in North Africa, Germany occupied the southern sector of France, hitherto governed by the collaborationist Vichy government, the Italians were given control of eight French departments, frequently frustrating the viciously anti-Semitic actions of the French authorities by their relatively moderate policies.

From early 1941, Monsignor O'Flaherty toured prisoner-of-war camps in Italy as secretary-interpreter to the papal nuncio, attempting to discover news about Allied prisoners reported missing in action, mainly during the desert war in North Africa. He created lists of prisoners and, with a New Zealand-born colleague, Father Owen Snedden, broadcast the information gathered over Vatican Radio in an effort to bring some comfort to their families. O'Flaherty organized the distribution of Red Cross parcels in the internment camps and disseminated some 10,000 books, together with quantities of a prayer book he had compiled and printed. At Modena and Piacenza the forceful Monsignor was even able to get two particularly unpleasant camp commandants removed.[1] Around Christmas 1942 he was forced to cease his POW camp activities after pressure from the Italian Fascist authorities.

---

1   John Furman, *Be Not Fearful*, Anthony Blond, London, 1959, p. 93.

Monsignor Hugh O'Flaherty
Copyright © O'Flaherty Family Archives

Ten days after the historic Wannsee Conference in Berlin in January 1942, where it was decided that the Final Solution should be implemented, Hitler had made a speech threatening that '[t]he Jews will be liquidated for at least a thousand years!' But Pope Pius XII and his advisor Cardinal Maglione were preoccupied with saving Christianity from Communism and the city of Rome from destruction by Allied bombing. Konrad

Pope Pius XII
Wiki commons

von Preysing, Catholic Bishop of Berlin, wrote to Pius in 1943 saying that, terrible as the Allied bombing of Berlin was, what was happening to Berlin's Jews was infinitely worse. Pius responded by claiming that he sympathized with the Jews but would do nothing that might threaten Rome, because Christians regarded the city as the centre of Christendom. Meanwhile, he did little enough for the Jews privately or clandestinely.

By contrast, we know that Angelo Giuseppe Roncalli, the future Pope John XXIII, 'made representations and protests, issued false baptismal papers [and] helped Jews escape' as a diplomat in the Balkans and Near East until 1944, and then as papal nuncio to France.[2] The strenuous efforts of the Vatican to prevent an 'atrocity' in Rome compared with its silence about atrocities elsewhere in Europe provoked d'Arcy Osborne to declare in December 1942: 'The more I think of it, the more I am revolted by Hitler's massacre of the Jewish race on the one hand, and . . . the Vatican's apparently exclusive preoccupation with the effects of the war on Italy and the possibilities of the bombardment of Rome.'

Hugh O'Flaherty was a fiercely nationalist Irishman. The bitterly fought Irish War of Independence and Irish Civil War had taken place less than 20 years earlier and many Catholic priests supported the Republicans, while the neutrality of Éire during the Second World War fomented huge resentment in Britain. Early in the Second World War O'Flaherty had declared, 'I don't think there's anything to choose between Britain and Germany.'

One experience that helped change O'Flaherty's mind was the treatment of Jews in Rome. In June 1942 a Rome newspaper published a front-page photograph of Jewish forced labour on the banks of the River Tiber. When asked by Major Derry why he was helping now, O'Flaherty said:

Well, I will tell you, me boy. When this war started I used to listen to broadcasts from both sides. All propaganda,

2 Irving Greenberg, 'Cloud of Smoke, Pillar of Fire', in *Holocaust: Religious and philosophical implications*, ed. J. K. Roth and M. Berenbaum, Paragon, New York, 1989, p. 313.

of course, and both making the same terrible charges against the other. I frankly didn't know which side to believe – until they started rounding up the Jews in Rome. They treated them like beasts, making old men and respectable women get down on their knees and scrub the roads. You know the sort of thing that happened after that; it got worse and worse, and I knew then which side I had to believe.

Matters changed drastically on 10 July 1943, when the Allies landed on the island of Sicily, in southernmost Italy, two days after Italy had surrendered to them. Germany took over Italy's military bases, seized control of Rome and disarmed most of the Italian forces. For the Jews of Italy, things instantly changed for the worse.

In Rome the Germans installed a Gestapo chief named Herbert Kappler, instructing him to prioritize the deportation of the city's Jews. But Kappler believed that to deport the Jews would further alienate the local population, who were already angered by the German occupation. He also told Berlin that he had insufficient military resources and experience to effect a major deportation. Instead, Kappler threatened the leaders of Rome's Jewish community that 200 Jews would be sent to Germany unless they handed over 50 kg of gold within 36 hours, apparently hoping this might delay the deportations. The treasure demanded from the city's 12,000-strong Jewish community was handed over – including gold tooth fillings – yet within hours the SS had raided the offices of the Jewish community, stealing money and documents, antiquarian manuscripts and rare books. Although Kappler apparently still hoped he could prevent or delay the deportations, he was ordered by *Obergrup-penführer* Ernst Kaltenbrunner to 'proceed with the evacuation of the Jews without further delay' in order to effect 'the immediate and thorough eradication of the Jews in Italy'.

In the first week of October SS Captain Dannecker, who the previous year had efficiently organized the mass round-ups of Jews in Paris, was sent to Rome to speed things along, accompanied by a detachment of the Waffen-SS. Kappler handed over a complete list of the names and addresses of Rome's Jews. Early on the morning of 16 October, SS officers and military policemen made a concerted raid on the city's Jewish ghetto. Every Jewish family was presented with a document in Italian and German, reading as follows:

1 You and your family and all other Jews belonging to your household are to be transferred.
2 You are to bring with you:
    - food for at least eight days
    - ration books
    - identity card
    - drinking glasses.
3 You may also bring:
    - a small suitcase with personal effects, clothing, blankets, etc.
    - money and jewellery.

Close and lock the flat/house. Take the key with you.
Invalids, even the severest cases, may not for any reason, stay behind. There are infirmaries at the camp.
Twenty minutes after presentation of this card, the family must be ready to depart.

The wording of this document was designed to give the impression that their destination would be safe and life would continue more or less as normal. Troops herded into open army trucks 1,259 people, many still in their nightclothes. They first gathered them near Rome's Teatro Marcello and then took them to the Italian Military College in Via della Lungara. At dawn the next day, after ID cards had been examined, couples in mixed marriages and Gentiles arrested in error were released. Finally, on 19 October, the remaining prisoners were loaded into 18 goods trucks at Tiburtina Station and dispatched to Auschwitz. Of the 1,030 who departed, 17 returned after the war.[3]

This was an action of which the British were well aware, as recent publication of an Ultra intercept of the German report, made at Bletchley Park, reveals:

Action against Jews started and finished today in accordance with a plan worked out as well as possible by the office . . . Participation of the Italian police was not possible in view of unreliability in this respect, as only possible by individual arrests in quick succession inside the 26 action districts. To cordon off whole blocks of streets, in view both of [Rome's] character as an open city and of the insufficient number of German police 365 in all, not practicable. In spite of this 1,259 persons were arrested in Jewish homes, and taken to assembly camp of the military school here in the course of the action which lasted from 0530 to 1400 hours. After

---

3 The names and ages of the passengers who did not return and the handful who did are recorded in Robert Katz, *Black Sabbath: A journey through a crime against humanity*, Arthur Barker, London, 1969, pp. 331–41.

the release of those of mixed blood, of foreigners including a Vatican citizen, of the families in mixed marriages including the Jewish partner, and of Aryan servants and lodgers there remain 1,002 Jews to be detained.

Such intercepts, however, though invaluable as information, rarely led to immediate intervention both for tactical reasons and also to protect this vital secret intelligence source.

The pope made no public condemnation of this raid. When the Germans occupied Rome, the Holy See feared for the sovereignty of Vatican City and the personal safety of the pope. Yet the Nazis were anxious to maintain cordial relations with the Holy See and, shortly before the 16 October round-up, asked the Vatican to confirm that the conduct of German occupation forces in Rome had been 'correct'. Pius issued the requested 'good conduct' letter and made no criticism of the deportation of the Jews. When the German ambassador, Ernst von Weizsäcker (whose son Richard later became German president), enquired what the Vatican would do if such raids continued, Cardinal Maglione responded, 'The Holy See would not wish to be put in a situation where it was necessary to utter a word of disapproval.' The pope and officials at the Vatican Secretariat of State seem to have been vaguely aware of the clandestine activities of Osborne and O'Flaherty, but turned a blind eye to them.[4]

Following this mass round-up, arrests of Jews in Rome continued, but in a less systematic manner. For the next

---

4 The Vatican is due to release documents in 2020 that may shed further light on the actions of Pius XII.

nine months Rome's Jews were constantly looking over their
shoulder. The remaining Jews began new lives in hiding places
they found across the city, as most had abandoned their own
homes in fear of further deportations. Some sought sanctuary
in the homes of friends, some in church properties, while
others fled the city to hide in villages and farm buildings.
Among the shelters were many institutions of the Roman
Catholic Church, including boarding schools, hospitals, convents, monasteries and even Vatican properties.

The October deportations greatly angered Monsignor
O'Flaherty – 'these gentle people [are] being treated like
beasts' he said – and marked a turning point in his view
of the war. He had moved from neutrality at the beginning of
the conflict to sympathy with the Allies and finally to actively
willing the defeat of the Germans. The arrest of so many Jews
also helped O'Flaherty's growing escape organization, as
it made it easier for him to secure the support of ordinary
Romans, who hitherto had been relatively indifferent to the
Germans. Some Vatican personnel were also prepared to
allow the Monsignor to continue his concealment and escape
efforts unhindered, despite their jeopardizing the church's
neutrality.

Monsignor O'Flaherty found accommodation for some
Jews in buildings owned by the church, and helped others
flee Italy. One German Jewish family apparently approached
him on the steps of St Peter's itself, desperately fearful they
were to be deported. They offered the priest a gold chain and
asked him to ensure the safety of their seven-year-old son.
O'Flaherty did better: he obtained false identity papers for
the boy's parents, who continued to live in the city using these

documents, and found their son a place of sanctuary. The family were reunited after the war.[5]

About 40 Jews, of whom at least 15 were Christian converts, seem to have been concealed in apartments belonging to individual prelates within the walls of Vatican City, while many more were hidden in Vatican properties outside its walls, scattered throughout Rome. These included some 55 Jews hidden at the Pontificio Seminario Romano Maggiore, near the Basilica di San Giovanni in Laterano, and 63 at the Seminario Lombardo, near the Basilica of Santa Maria Maggiore.

Under the terms of Italy's Armistice with the Allies, all prisoners of war were to be released, which set loose thousands of soldiers who then tried to rejoin the advancing Allied army. With Germany having rapidly occupied Italy, however, these men stood in imminent danger of recapture. The Vatican was a neutral state, with a duty under international law to intern escaped prisoners. But the British minister d'Arcy Osborne was determined to help them, energetically assisted by Hugh O'Flaherty, though lacking both money and agents.

From inside the Vatican, O'Flaherty began to construct a network of diplomats, priests and officials to help shelter escaped British, Russian, Polish and American POWs, Italian partisans, Jews and other refugees, and to create escape routes for them. His office was situated in the *Collegium Teutonicum*, the German College, behind the Holy Office – outside the Vatican State but extraterritorial, so not subject to the Italian police. Gestapo agents now operated in the Vatican and also ran Italian agents, but did not control the pontifical gendarmes.

---

5   Sam Derry, *The Rome Escape Line*, Harrap, London, 1960, p. 80.

With care and using a variety of disguises, O'Flaherty smuggled Allied troops on the run into the British Legation to meet Osborne.

When the Nazis started to transport more Jews from Rome to transit camps, O'Flaherty led them through the streets of Rome in small groups to places of concealment and provided them with fake Vatican papers for their safe passage. He smuggled out Jewish people disguised as nuns and monks, passed partisans off as Swiss guards, and found hiding places for hundreds of prisoners of war seeking sanctuary.

Like O'Flaherty, Osborne was scandalized when Jews in Rome were rounded up and made to scrub roads. Although he was actively helping to protect and hide escaped prisoners, he made every effort not to appear to be involved. It was vital that he avoid appearing to abuse his diplomatic privilege: 'I must not be seen to compromise the tacit conditions under which I am here in the Vatican State.' He took careful precautions, such as not dating letters in case they were discovered by the Germans, and pretended not to notice when O'Flaherty held escape meetings in his residence. As increasing numbers of British POWs sought refuge in the Vatican, the papacy grew increasingly concerned about its neutrality.

D'Arcy Osborne and O'Flaherty attempted to put the 'escape line' on a more sustainable and organized footing. Osborne adopted the code name 'Mount' and supported the efforts with his own money. The urbane ambassador also lent the services of his butler, a cockney named John May with many contacts in the black market. Hugh O'Flaherty reckoned him the 'most magnificent scrounger who ever lived', while May described O'Flaherty as one as the most charismatic men he had met.

Thousands of prisoners were spirited away. Ordinary men and women risked everything to hide POWs ranging from privates to generals. Rescuers included a Maltese widow named Henrietta Chevalier, whose daughters danced to gramophone records in order to drown the sound of their frequent 'guests'. She also arranged for black-market supplies to be smuggled around the city to feed the fugitives.

O'Flaherty recruited the help of several other priests, including two young New Zealanders, Fathers Owen Snedden and John Flanagan, two agents working with the Free French, François de Vial and Yves Debroise, some communists and a Swiss count. Another vital supporter was the British Major Sam Derry.[6] Derry kept careful records of both prisoners and money, burying his files in biscuit tins in the Vatican gardens. Other escaping POWs – the Scots Lieutenant Bill Simpson and Jewish Lieutenant John Furman, both of whom spoke Italian, and Canadian Captain Byrnes – were responsible for security and operations, daily braving Nazi patrols to distribute supplies and money. Bill Simpson, a Presbyterian Christian, called Hugh his 'favourite hero', and claimed he never tried to ram God down anyone's throat.

Priests, nuns and lay people worked secretly with O'Flaherty, some even hiding Jewish refugees in their own homes, among them Augustinian Maltese Fathers Egidio Galea, Aurelio Borg and Ugolino Gatt, the Dutch Augustinian Father Anselmus Musters and Brother Robert Pace of the Brothers of Christian Schools.

6　For a concise and objective summary of Sam Derry's work, see M. R. D. Foot and J. M. Langley, *MI9: Escape and evasion 1939–1945*, Biteback, London, 2011, pp. 180–5.

'Time after time, Monsignor came to our Franciscan Generalate, located at that time in the Via Nicola Fabrizio on the Gianiculum,' remembered Sister Noreen Dennehy, a Franciscan missionary. 'He often asked us to house the persecuted Jews . . . we were able to accommodate as many as fourteen or fifteen at any one time.' Ines Ghiron, a Jewish refugee in Rome, recounted the following:

> Monsignor O'Flaherty placed me and my Jewish friend – Rose-Mary Roth from Yugoslavia – in a *pensione* run by Canadian nuns at Monteverde. We were given false IDs. We lived with elderly women in the guesthouse, strictly separated from the enclosed nuns. After the Nazis began searching for Jews, the *pensione* became so full of Jewish refugees that the Pope ordered the enclosed area to be opened up so as to take in as many refugees as possible. I gave up my room to a woman with two children and went to live in a very small cell within the enclosed area.[7]

Jewish religious services were held in the Basilica di San Clemente, which was under Irish diplomatic protection, beneath a painting of Tobias, the righteous Israelite whose story is told in the Book of Tobit in the deuterocanonical Bible.

Almost all the civilians whom O'Flaherty assisted were Italians, and many were Jewish. The Jewish people in Rome also had their own welfare organization, DELASEM, whose president by the autumn of 1943 was Father Marie-Benoît

---

7   Margherita Marchione, *Yours Is a Precious Witness: Memoirs of Jews and Catholics in wartime Italy*, Paulist Press, New York/Mahwah, NJ, 1997, p. 73; *La Repubblica*, 27 April 1986, p. 8.

(1895–1990), a Capuchin Franciscan friar. He had come to Rome from Nice, where previously he had befriended Jews. 'I was the only committee member sufficiently unknown in the city to be able to go about freely,' Benoît explained. Initially he was preoccupied with finding accommodation in Italy for Jews fleeing Nice, but from September 1943 he extended his work to Italian Jews.[8]

Until the winter of 1943 it had been official policy to refuse asylum in the Vatican to political dissidents, escaped Allied prisoners of war and Jews. However, as Italian hostility towards the Germans increased, enforcement softened. In all around 160 political refugees and Jews entered the Vatican unofficially, along with a few escaped Allied prisoners of war sponsored by individual priests. The pope and the Vatican Secretariat of State turned a blind eye to the activities of d'Arcy Osborne, Hugh O'Flaherty and the other helpers.

In January 1944, in his official role, O'Flaherty encountered the German ambassador, von Weizsäcker, at a reception in the Hungarian Embassy. The diplomat informed O'Flaherty that the Germans knew of the escape organization and that he would be arrested if he left the Vatican. Herbert Kappler, head of the Gestapo in Rome, had a white line painted across the pavement of St Peter's Square, marking the boundary between Vatican City and Italy, and warned O'Flaherty that he would be executed if he crossed it. Kappler was said to have become obsessed with trapping the Irishman, and made several vain attempts to hustle him over this border.

---

8 For a full account, see Susan Zuccotti, *Père Marie-Benoît and Jewish Rescue*, Indiana University Press, Bloomington and Indianapolis, 2013.

Outwith the safety of the Vatican, O'Flaherty often resorted to disguise. He once dressed as a coalman to evade a Nazi raid on the Palazzo Doria Pamphili, when visiting one of his strongest supporters, the staunchly anti-Fascist Prince Don Filippo Andrea VI Doria-Pamphili-Landi. He is even rumoured to have dressed as a nun on another occasion. Inevitably, he became dubbed Rome's 'Scarlet Pimpernel'.

Some of O'Flaherty's helpers were executed for their under-ground work, including five in the appalling massacre at the Ardeatine Caves, on the outskirts of Rome, where the Germans executed 335 men in a single night in retaliation for a partisan attack on 22 March 1944 that had killed 33 Nazi soldiers. Executing ten prisoners for every German soldier killed in the original explosion, the Germans cold-bloodedly shot them in the caves before setting off explosives to seal the bodies inside. Those slaughtered included 75 Jews. This dread-ful act provoked massive ill feeling in Rome.

Monsignor O'Flaherty's group continued their work until the Allies liberated Rome in June 1944, only nine months after Italy had surrendered. Of the 9,700 Jews in Rome in 1943, 1,007 had been shipped to Auschwitz. Michael Tagliacozzo, who survived the 1943 round-up, estimated that 447 Jews were concealed in the Vatican and a further 4,238 in monasteries and convents throughout Rome, but it is difficult to be confident about these figures. From the whole of Italy, some 7,000 Jews were deported and killed. More than 80 per cent of Italian Jews survived, mainly in hiding or by fleeing to neutral Switzerland.

When peace came, O'Flaherty demanded that German prisoners be treated correctly. The British refused to allow Jews from Rome to travel to Palestine, but O'Flaherty worked

**Memorial at the entrance to the Ardeatine Caves,
site of a terrible massacre**
Wiki commons formkurve

with contacts in DELASEM, funds from the USA and the
Jewish underground *Haganah* organization to acquire boats
to transport them,[9] and flew to the Holy Land to visit Jewish
refugees in Jerusalem.[10]

9 Gordon Thomas, *The Pope's Jews*, The Robson Press, London, 2013, p. 272.

10 Brian Fleming, *The Vatican Pimpernel: The wartime exploits of Monsignor Hugh
O'Flaherty*, Collins Press, Cork, 2008, p. 174.

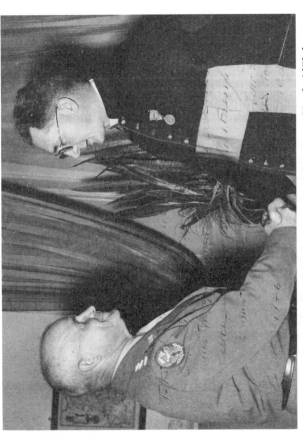

Lieutenant General John C. H. Lee presents Monsignor Hugh O'Flaherty
with the US Medal of Freedom, Rome 1946

After the war, Sam Derry was recruited by British intelligence, while on 7 June 1944 Sir d'Arcy Osborne was officially thanked at Westminster for serving for 'a prolonged period of exceptional difficulty under conditions that must be unique in diplomatic experience'.

Herbert Kappler, the Gestapo colonel who had tried to capture O'Flaherty, was convicted of war crimes and sentenced to life imprisonment. The Monsignor was one of the few people to visit his old foe in the Regina Coeli Prison in Rome, and in 1959 he helped him convert to the Roman Catholic faith. Monsignor O'Flaherty was awarded the CBE and the US Medal of Freedom with Silver Palm, but was not greatly approved of in the post-war Vatican. He suffered a stroke in 1960 and, after a brief term in the US Archdiocese of Southern California, returned to Ireland to live with his sister in Cahersiveen, County Kerry, where he died on 30 October 1963 aged 65.

In O'Flaherty's home town of Killarney stands a bronze statue by Alan Ryan Hall on which appears his aphorism 'God has no country', while a grove of trees dedicated to his memory was planted in Killarney National Park. There is an active campaign to have Hugh O'Flaherty recognized as one of the Righteous Among the Nations.

9

Committed Swedes

PASTORS ERIK PERWE AND
ERIK MYRGREN, BERLIN

Sweden, like Switzerland, was neutral in the Second World War, but allowed the Germans to move military supplies and thousands of troops across its territory and supplied warships to the Third Reich. Yet a small Swedish Lutheran church in Berlin was served by three successive pastors who committed themselves to helping the city's persecuted Jews in various – sometimes ingenious – ways, and constantly put themselves in the way of danger.

Erik Myrgren (1914–96) had no intention of staying in Berlin in November 1944: it was merely a convenient stopover. The war was entering its final dangerous phase and the 30-year-old Swedish pastor was on his way home to celebrate Christmas with his wife and young daughter. His ministry to sailors in the Baltic city of Stettin (today Szczecin, Poland) had shrivelled away, both because Swedish ships were no longer calling there and because the Allies had bombed his church, and he was booked to fly home to neutral Stockholm. Instead, as acting head of the Swedish church in Berlin, he spent the next six months attempting to outsmart the Nazis in Hitler's capital, the last hope for some of the remnant of Jews who had managed to evade the last five years' searches, denunciations, deportations and murders.

Although it was now clear that the war had been lost, the Gestapo was if anything even more menacing. When war broke out in 1939, the Jewish population of Berlin was estimated at 75,500. By mid-June 1943, Goebbels had managed to deport most of Berlin's Jews to Auschwitz, where at least half were killed on arrival, and Hitler's propaganda maestro is said to have declared Berlin *Judenrein* (free of Jews). Yet 6,700 Jews were still living legally in the city, most of them married to Christians and in theory not liable to deportation. By the time the Nazis surrendered in 1945, just 4,700 Jews married to Aryans remained in Berlin, while a further 1,400 Jews survived in hiding.

Berlin's Swedish Victoria Church had been founded in the Wilmersdorf district in 1903. In 1929 Revd Birger Forell (1893–1958) succeeded as pastor of this church, based at Landhausstrasse 27, a large villa that had been converted to serve as a church, school and parsonage, and of which only the bell tower now remains. From the outset Forell had a particular concern for his neediest parishioners, and as Hitler rose to power the parish began to forge contacts with the German Confessing Church.[1] Forell used both his diplomatic privilege and contacts outside Germany to help victims of persecution flee the country, while also reporting back to Sweden on developments within Germany.

Forell's successor, Erik Perwe (1905–44), continued his work and expanded the rescue network. In 1935 the Swedish

---

1 See p. 134, footnote 6 for a brief description of the Confessing Church.

**The Swedish Victoria Church,
Landhausstrasse 27, Berlin**

Mission for Israel (*Svenska Israelsmissionens*) had sent Pastor
Göte Hedenqvist (1907–96) to Vienna in response to a request
from the Austrian Evangelical Church to help baptize Jews
threatened by Nazi persecution. Possession of a baptism certificate was accepted as proof of Christian identity by some
neighbouring countries, thus allowing Jewish refugees entry.
Hedenqvist had decided he should make no distinction

between baptized and non-baptized Jews and issued a baptism certificate to any who requested it. As a result of his efforts, it is estimated that between 1935 and 1939 some 1,000 Jewish children and 2,000 adults were able to leave Austria.[2] In the autumn of 1935 Erik Perwe visited Vienna, Bratislava and Berlin to observe the work of the Swedish mission, revisiting Vienna for a month in 1938. The young pastor was appalled by the treatment of Jews that he witnessed in Berlin and spoke out publicly about it on his return home. Perwe's work was noted by Archbishop Erling Eidem (1880–1972), who sent him to Berlin in March 1939 as a locum for Forell.[3] Perwe was shocked by the indifference to Jewish oppression that he discovered among his Lutheran colleagues in Germany.

Revd Forell had set up an information and support network linked to the Grüber Office (*Büro Grüber*), initiated in September 1938 by the Berlin Confessing Church pastor Heinrich Grüber (1891–1975) to help Christians of Jewish origin emigrate from Germany.[4] Grüber had already been helping Jewish Christians for several years, together with Confessing Church members such as Marga Meusel and Martin Albertz. When Jewish children were barred from German schools, they set up informal classes for them in some parishes. Forell was also in touch with Laura Livingstone, Bishop George Bell's sister-in-law, who went to Berlin in July 1937 as representative of the International Christian Committee for German

---

2 See Chapter 2, where the similar efforts of Revds Grimes and Collard in Vienna are described.

3 Until late in the war the archbishop spoke out only once, and then in general terms, in protest against German anti-Semitism, ostensibly for fear of infringing Sweden's neutrality.

4 By 1939 its office was at An der Stechbahn 3/4, Berlin.

Refugees and worked out of the Quaker offices there. Working with the *Hilfsverein* and the Quaker Refugee Committee, Miss Livingstone apparently confronted Adolf Eichmann several times concerning exit permits for her clients.[5] With his secretary, Sylvia Wolff, Forell helped some 200 Christians of Jewish origin emigrate to Sweden.

In April 1942 Forell was expelled by the Nazis as an 'undesirable' for his efforts to protect Jews.[6] Myrgren later described him as 'a serious man . . . who did not like to joke . . . He had a great capacity for work and was very courageous'. As we have seen, Pastor Forell had previously introduced Perwe to his work, and in early September 1942 the latter was appointed pastor of the Swedish Victoria church and moved to Berlin with his wife and four children. 'God calls: I must obey,' he wrote in his diary.

Perwe proceeded to build a comprehensive relief network in an attempt to protect Jews from deportation. Like Dr Abegg,[7] he was fully aware of, and wanted to help, the many 'underground' Jews in Berlin who were desperately trying to survive.[8] Despite the fact that in June 1943 Berlin was declared *Judenrein*, many Jewish 'submarines' remained in the city and were in desperate need of help. Perwe and his church played an important role in this work. As in Vienna, Paris and Budapest, Perwe created fake baptismal certificates to help provide 'Aryan' ID for some of the 'U-boats'. Perwe also had strong support from church staff such as the parish nurses, Vide Ohmann

---

5 Laura Livingstone became the first woman relief worker to enter Bergen-Belsen camp after its liberation in 1945.

6 A monument commemorating his work is located at Landhausstrasse 26, Berlin-Wilmersdorf.

7 See Chapter 5.

8 See Chapter 5 for a description of the Jewish 'U-boats'.

and Meri Siöcrona, and Eric Wesslén (1918–64), an enterprising young man who used his contacts with the Gestapo to 'purchase' freedom for some Jewish fugitives.

Perwe was well aware that he was under surveillance. He occasionally had visitors who he guessed had probably been sent by the Gestapo, and lived in constant fear that one of his team might be arrested and under torture would reveal the entire enterprise. The head of the Swedish Legation in Berlin, Arvid Richert (1887–1981), gave Perwe unofficial support, but warned that he could not assist him should he be arrested. Perwe reported on the Jews' terrible situation and appealed for official action in a letter to Archbishop Erling Eidem, whom he had known since student days, but in vain. Outwardly, Perwe played his role as a clergyman from a neutral country and was frequently invited to diplomatic receptions where he met Nazi Party officials.

Supported by devoted staff and German friends, and equipped with money for bribes, Perwe turned his church compound into a haven for Jewish fugitives. As early as 1938 Pastor Forell had constructed two secret rooms in the church attic, where fugitive Jews could hide during the day. Although the church's entrance on Landhausstrasse was often guarded by the Gestapo, there was also a concealed way in from Kaiserallee through the garden. Perwe started to collect the ration coupons necessary to purchase groceries for the fugitives, forged baptism certificates and allowed a grumpy Jewish violinist from Leipzig named Erich Müller to live in the attic. By bribing airline and railway officials, he arranged for many Jewish fugitives to travel to neutral Sweden. Air raids were destroying many potential hiding places, and Perwe allowed increasing numbers of fugitives to sleep in the church

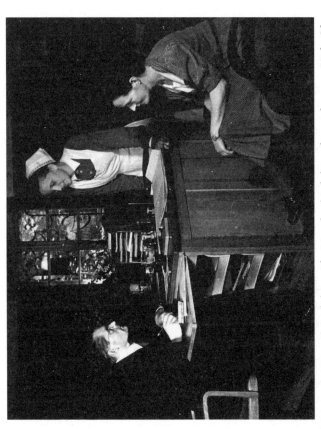

Erik Perwe (1905–44) with his wife, Martha (right), and parish nurse Vide Ohmann

By kind permission of Johann Perwe and the Silent Heroes Memorial Center, Berlin

basement. For others he provided the money, food, false documents and other forms of support necessary for them to hide as 'submarines'. Sister Vide recalled in 1987:

We were aware that many people – mainly Jews – came to speak to Erik Perwe. They found him in his office or in the church forecourt, where he often used to repair or clean the car . . . He told us not to question, not to act on our own and never to reveal what we had heard or seen or taken part in.

Pastor Perwe kept a diary, with brief, laconic entries chronicling his daily affairs and visitors. The following extracts illustrate some of the problems he faced:

21 October 1942: Mrs. Ida Kuransky, concerning her child whom she wishes to send to Sweden.

31 October 1942: A woman, Jewish, with two small, star-marked girls.[9] Wanted to have the children adopted in Sweden.

17 November 1942: A woman concerning the Swedish Red Cross's relationship with Theresienstadt, to which her mother had been deported.

18 November 1942: Received as a guest for a few days Miss Rubin, Jewish, who is bound for Sweden.

---

9   That is, with the yellow Star of David.

11 December 1942: Received word that the German author Klepper took his, his wife's and daughter's life last night. His wife and daughter had been threatened with deportation . . .[10]

12 December 1942: Car to Tempelhof [airport] with Miss Jenny Rubin, who happily moves to Sweden.

16 December 1942: Supper with Bishop Meiser.[11] Interesting man but exceptionally careful.
[Bishop Meiser gave Perwe three pieces of advice: 'One: Be careful. Two: Be careful. Three: Be careful.' To which Perwe replied, 'I might just as well pack my bags and return to Sweden.']

28 December 1942: Many 'non-Aryans' because of the aggravated situation.

1 January 1943: Visit from a Jewish couple who needed housing . . .

4 January 1943: Many homeless Jews.

1 March 1943: [Allied] Air raid of worst kind. Three fire bombs in the house, one of which in my room in the

---

10 The Protestant author Jochen Klepper (1903–42), who was married to a Jewish woman named Johanna Stein. His older stepdaughter, Brigitte, emigrated safely to England in 1939. Birger Forell was shaken by these deaths: negotiations to enable the family to escape had been started more than a year earlier.

11 Hans Meiser (1881–1956), first *Landesbischof* of the Evangelical Lutheran Church of Bavaria.

apartment. The blue hundred-year-old sofa and a black table destroyed. We succeeded in the nick of time in dousing the flames. Berlin is a sea of fire.

2 March 1943: Worked at home preparing for air raids to come. God be with us!

5 March 1943: Martha and the children to Sweden. Sad but necessary. God protect them all!
[Perwe's family went home only after the church had been hit by bombs.]

7 March 1943: Worked late with Dr. Lehfeld on a report to the Swedish government re: persecution of Jews.

17 August 1943: Air raid. A terrible attack by 900 planes with 5,000 men . . .

22 November 1943: Air raid, the worst of them all. The home, Legation building in ruins, city in turmoil. Helped evacuate Legation. Then by car to the church. Three hours struggle against fire and smoke.

31 December 1943: So ends this year, a terrible year. May God have mercy on the deeds of this year, their perpetrators and their victims.

Among other helpers with whom Perwe cooperated was Maria Gräfin (Countess) von Maltzan (1909–97), an aristocrat who from as early as 1933 worked with anti-Nazi organizations in Germany. The youngest of seven siblings, Maria von Maltzan was born at Schloss Militsch (today Milicz, Poland) near Breslau, where her father was governor of Silesia. A life-long rebel, she was sent to a fashionable Berlin girls' boarding school popular with wealthy Jews, with whose daughters she became good friends. In 1932 Maltzan became involved with an anti-Nazi group in Munich organized by a Jesuit priest named Father Friedrich Muckermann, concerning which the Gestapo interrogated her more than once. Back in Berlin she started to train as a vet, while also rescuing underground Jews, helping them to find safe houses and acquire false IDs.

Von Maltzan played an important role in the rescue efforts of the Swedish Church, providing temporary shelter and Aryan documents for Jews in hiding. She said later:

> I had a good hairdresser. I got him to teach me how to do men's hair and beards. I could never let them go to the barber because that's where you sit for a long time and people talk. Many people were caught at the barber's . . . I was a queen of the black market throughout the war. I had to be good at it because I had so many extra people to feed. I always said, 'I prefer to be in a tough situation than go to bed with a bad conscience.'[12]

---

12 Von Maltzan complained that Leonard Gross, who wrote about her in *The Last Jews in Berlin* (Simon & Schuster, New York, 1982) and then made a film about her (*Forbidden*, starring Jacqueline Bisset), stole her story. She was also angry when Israel offered to make her one of the Righteous Among the Nations at a time when they were bombing Palestinian refugees: 'I'm furious with Israel. They wanted me to plant a eucalyptus tree and get a medal pinned on my breast. I really don't care for such things . . . I wrote back saying that all my life I've been for the peaceful coexistence of people of all colours and religions, and I don't think Israel has anything to do with my ideals. So I don't think I want to have a medal from you. I didn't go.'

Unloading aid packages from Sweden outside the Swedish Victoria church in Berlin-Wilmersdorf, 1944

By kind permission of Johann Perwe and the help of the Silent Heroes Memorial Center, Berlin

In October 1944 von Maltzan participated in a bold rescue plan by which 20 Jews were to be smuggled out of Berlin stowed in railway crates used by Swedes to ship their furniture home under diplomatic privilege. Erik Wesslén bribed *Reichsbahn* personnel, who agreed to stop the train a short distance outside Berlin, where the Jews would be loaded onto the train in place of the furniture, in an operation known as 'Swedish furniture' (*Schwedenmöbel*). Von Maltzan successfully guided the Jewish fugitives to the meeting point, but on the return journey she was trapped in woods by SS men with searchlights and dogs, and had to hide in a tree for a day and two nights before arriving back in Berlin on the verge of collapse.

Pastor Perwe planned to fly to Sweden for two weeks at the end of November 1944. Erik Myrgren had arrived in Berlin on 4 November after his church in Stettin had been destroyed by an Allied bomb the previous August. Perwe asked if he would cover for him while he was away. Myrgren immediately agreed, having as yet no clue about Perwe's undercover activities. Perwe accordingly flew home to Sweden on 29 November. Over the Baltic Sea, near Falsterbo, on the south-west tip of Sweden, his plane was shot down and all passengers killed. Rumours spread that the Gestapo had ordered the plane to be destroyed.

Initially, Myrgren was unaware that the Swedish church was being used as a refuge. When he discovered 15 people hiding in the basement, he felt completely unequipped for his new task. 'I was overcome by panic,' he wrote later. 'I knew so little about Perwe's work and practically nothing about his secret activities.' Over the next few nights, Perwe's 'submarines' started to surface at the church. Myrgren was haunted by what they told him. Ordained only two years earlier, he felt out of his depth.

A few weeks later Myrgren read from Isaiah at a Christmas service: 'The people that walked in darkness have seen a great light; they that dwell in the land of the shadow of death, upon them hath the light shined' (KJV). Suddenly he saw things in a different light:

It was as if the words left the page and entered the present reality. They had been changed into people I knew, events so terribly real. Everything was there: the sounds of war, the torture camps, the despair, the bloodshed, but also the beam of light, the hope of final victory and the love despite it all.

Now committed to continuing Perwe's mission, Myrgren became a different person: 'Slowly, I became part of the machine that Perwe . . . had built up so carefully.'

Myrgren's closest aide was Erik Wesslén, the young community worker, who had come to Berlin to study landscape gardening. He had already proved immensely helpful to Perwe and was a great fixer:

He had a good mind, was full of ideas, brave and adventurous. He bought cars for a few kilos of coffee, and managed to get coal for heating and petrol for the vehicles. He got building material and workers when things needed repairing. He even bribed guards and policemen to allow captured Jews to 'disappear'. It was a terrible – but necessary – business: buying people. Jews for coffee, alcohol, chocolate, money and jewels.

Myrgren shared Wesslén's youthful enthusiasm and things soon moved on. 'With others in the church . . . I did what had to be done. People needed help . . . Help with food and clothing, a place to hide, transport to a secure place, some money, maybe medical care or just some words of comfort and hope.' The Jewish fugitives Martin and Margot Weissenberg had been hiding in the church since being bombed out of an old people's home in March 1943, after having sent their children to safety in Britain. Myrgren learned how to get hold of ration cards and false papers and how to use church records to create counterfeit histories for illegals so they could obtain false ID cards.

Two unlikely allies were Sergeants Hoffman and Friedrich Mattick (1890–1945) from the police station situated opposite the church. These two passed on messages, kept spies away and warned the pastor if the Gestapo was approaching by lowering a blind at the police station. Mattick was an earthy Berliner and a committed Social Democrat who joked dangerously about 'the big guys up there' (*die Grossen da oben*), dismissing Goebbels' propaganda broadcasts as 'clubfooted fairy tales' (*lumpische Märchenstunden*).

With the help of German transport officials angling for favourable post-war treatment, Pastor Myrgren managed to get many Jews out of the country by sea via the port of Lübeck and by plane from Tempelhof Airport. Mattick obtained fake Swedish passports for Martin and Margot Weissenberg in the name of Berg, stamped with genuine permits to depart. Myrgren and Wesslén drove them to Tempelhof Airport to catch one of the last flights to Stockholm, but – even with the correct papers – their departure was fraught with danger.

When the registration office in one Berlin district was bombed, the German authorities told people to bring any identification they possessed to obtain new documents. A Jewish woman asked Myrgren if he could give her the name of a Swedish woman born in Berlin about the same time as her but who had returned to Sweden. The pastor found such a name in the church records and wrote a note to confirm she was this woman. Years later she wrote to Myrgren from the USA thanking him for saving her life.

In December 1944 Myrgren took in Wolfgang Hammerschmidt (1925–2006), post-war chief dramaturge of the East Berlin *Komische Oper* (Comic Opera), whom the Gestapo were pursuing after he had escaped from a labour camp. 'I was kindly received,' he recalled later; 'given a sleeping bag, allowed to stay in the refectory and was well fed.' Of Pastor Myrgren he wrote, 'While many strangers listened anxiously by candlelight to the howling and exploding bombs, the young pastor sang Swedish songs quietly on his guitar . . . In the two weeks I was allowed to spend there, I felt I recovered as never before.'

Myrgren soon realized that not every visitor could be taken at face value. A tall blond man came asking for help, claiming to be an Orthodox Jew. The pastor had learned some Hebrew at seminary so asked him to recite a Jewish blessing, but the man couldn't manage even the opening words. In March 1945 a Jewish man who talked his way in was smuggled to Sweden by bus. 'I discovered years later this man was an informer,' Myrgren recalled. 'It pains me to this day.'

In February 1945 Himmler agreed that the Red Cross could evacuate Scandinavians held in concentration camps in 'white buses'. The Berlin collection point was the Swedish Church, and, using fake papers, Myrgren and Wesslén were able to put a number of German Jews on the buses. Meri Siöcrona escorted the passengers safely to the port of Lübeck, whence they sailed on to Sweden. This operation was fraught with danger, as the Gestapo randomly checked passports. Here again Mattick's help was invaluable, since he informed Myrgren when checks were likely to happen.

There were plenty of disappointments. For many Jewish 'U-boats', help came too late. Others were arrested on their way to freedom. On 2 May 1945 Berlin surrendered. Sadly, the courageous Friedrich Mattick had been killed by a bomb the previous day. Three days later Russian soldiers set fire to the Swedish Church. Myrgren and his team sought sanctuary in the Swedish Legation until they could be evacuated home. The pastor settled with his family in a remote rural parish in Sweden. He had one further foreign mission, supervising a prisoner exchange during the Korean War. 'It was exciting,' he said, 'but you couldn't compare it with Berlin.'

In 1987, Erik Myrgren was named as one of Israel's Righteous Among the Nations. At the ceremony in Jerusalem he said:

I feel very humble, and surely I am not worthy of being honoured with such an outstanding distinction. Whatever I did during my time in Berlin, I never felt there was anything special about it. On the contrary, I always felt that it wasn't enough. I simply tried as best I could to do what my sainted parents taught me: 'Help your fellow man, whoever he is and whatever he needs.'

Pastor Myrgren died on 20 October 1996 at Hörby, Sweden. The efforts of Pastors Forell, Perwe and Myrgren were heroic in a period during which the Swedish church and the government have been accused of inaction and silence. How many Jews they saved it is impossible to know.

10

An elusive missionary

ELSIE TILNEY, VITTEL

Elsie Tilney devoted most of her life to Christian missions to the Jews, while her brother, Dr Frederick Tilney, a homeopathic practitioner, devised a health and fitness regime for Angelo Siciliano (1892–1972), better known as bodybuilder Charles Atlas. Elsie's love for the Jewish people led to practical support for them prior to the Second World War and great bravery while she was interned as a foreign national in France during the conflict.

Elsie Maude Tilney was born in Norwich in 1893 into a Nonconformist family and in 1903 she joined Surrey Street Chapel, Norwich, an independent evangelical Nonconformist church with a Sunday school numbering 600 children. 'A pretty young lady with a sweet mellow voice', in 1919 Elsie was accepted to serve with the Mildmay Mission to the Jews, with its proselytizing motto 'to the Jew first'.[1]

---

1 'For I am not ashamed of the gospel of Christ: for it is the power of God unto salvation to every one that believeth; to the Jew first, and also to the Greek,' Romans 1.16–17, KJV.

Elsie then spent spells in Algeria and Tunisia working with the North Africa Mission, and spoke of the love shown to her by some of the Jewish families she was attempting to evangelize. As early as 1933 the pastor of her supportive home church in Norwich, Revd David Panton (1870–1955), wrote an article denouncing Hitler's 'anti-Semitic fury', hatred which he defined as 'purely racial and fanatical'.

In 1934 Miss Tilney moved from Djerba, Tunisia, to Paris, working again with the North Africa Mission. By 1936 she was based at the Église Evangélique Baptiste at 123 avenue du Maine in Paris' 14th arrondissement, where she 'was privileged to help and witness to the suffering German Jewish refugees', possibly mainly among children. Miss Tilney told her friends and supporters back in Norwich that the French pastor, Henri Vincent, threw open 'his church – and heart – to Jewish people'. In Paris she also worked alongside a church deacon named André Frankl (1895–1964), whose grandfather had been a Hungarian rabbi, and who was supported by the American Board of Missions to the Jews. The Paris Baptist Church offered practical help, including a daily soup kitchen for Jewish migrants from Germany and Austria, many of them doctors and teachers. As in Vienna, Hungary and Berlin, the Baptist pastor also offered baptism and an appropriate certificate to Jewish refugees as a means of acquiring a 'Christian' ID.

In 1939, at a time when Viennese Jews were being rounded up by the Nazis,[2] Elsie Tilney took the huge risk of collecting one-year-old baby Ruth Buchholz from her Jewish mother, Rita, at Vienna's Westbahnhof Station and delivering

---

2   See Chapter 2.

Elsie Tilney (1893–1974)
Courtesy Norwich Record Office

her to relative safety with her father, Leon, at the Gare de l'Est in Paris on 23 July, leaving him with her name and Norwich address pencilled on a scrap of paper: 'Miss E. M. Tilney, "Menuka", Blue Bell Road, Norwich, *Angleterre*'. Elsie Tilney had also intended to bring back Rita's 11-year-old cousin Herta, but at the last minute her mother couldn't face parting from her. In October 1941 mother and daughter were deported to the Łódź ghetto, where both were killed. For more than 60 years Leon treasured the slip of paper with Tilney's address, and after his death the yellowing fragment fell from an old suitcase while his son, human rights lawyer Philippe Sands, was researching his family history. Elsie's action almost certainly saved the life of Ruth Buchholz, Professor Sands' mother.[3]

Elsie continued her efforts in Paris, making several train journeys to accompany Jewish refugees to Le Havre and other French ports so that they could make their way to safety in the USA. When it became impossible to receive financial support from home, she relied on the American Embassy for help.

Following the German defeat and occupation of France in 1940, foreign nationals were sent to internment camps as 'enemy aliens'. Early in 1941 Elsie Tilney was dispatched with other British women to military barracks in Besançon, where they discovered appalling conditions: little food, filthy accommodation and severe overcrowding. In May she was transferred, with around 2,000 other women and children, to the German internment camp at Vittel, housed in ten requisitioned hotels surrounded by barbed-wire fences at least three

---

3   Philippe Sands, *East West Street*, Weidenfeld & Nicolson, London, 2017.

4214 VITTEL — LE GRAND HOTEL

1930s postcard of the Grand Hôtel, Vittel, France, which became part of Frontslag 121, where Elsie Tilney was interned

Wiki commons

metres high. *Frontslag* 121, as Vittel internment camp was known by the Germans, was located near Nancy, north-east France, in the spa town in the Vosges Mountains best known for its eponymous mineral water. Elsie was allocated to the Grand Hôtel, owned today by Club Med.

Vittel was a 'model' internment camp, housing mainly English-speaking people. Apart from deprivation of liberty and some discipline, the Vittel camp had little in common with most other concentration camps. It even had a little church where Catholic and Anglican priests were able to conduct services. The first large intake of Jewish prisoners to Vittel included several well-known rabbis, and Jewish holidays were observed. Josef Goebbels, Hitler's master propagandist, commissioned a film about Vittel in an effort to demonstrate to the world the supposedly humane conditions its internees enjoyed. This masked the cruel reality: Vittel was in fact a 'satellite' camp to Drancy on the outskirts of Paris, a transit centre for camps in the East.

An exotic internee named Sofka Skipwith, née Princess Sophia Dolgorouky (1907–94), described her experience of Vittel:

The rooms in the Grand Hôtel, where we were placed, ranged from large five- or six-bedded ones to singles, with running water, bathrooms on landings (some rooms had private baths of their own) in which we eventually achieved an occasional bath, and comfortable beds. The moment of arrival, however, was a shock. We entered the pillared hall and turned to make our way up the uncarpeted staircase. There in front of you was a large gilt-framed mirror reflecting the oddest looking creature, bedraggled, in a coat down to her ankles, hung about with tins and clutching several bundles. Suddenly it struck you with horror that you were staring at yourself.[4]

Mrs Skipwith seems initially almost to have enjoyed life in the Grand Hôtel:

People were allowed to receive parcels of things from Paris which were handed over after being examined by the guards in the parcels office; people were allowed to have money sent to them and any other amenities from home . . . The highbrows formed their own group round Sylvia Beach of the famous Shakespeare & Co. bookshop and publishers. Miss Derriman took over the Casino for cultural and educational pursuits, arranging lectures and classes. By the end of our stay it was so well organized that one could become proficient in several languages: English, French, German, Spanish or Russian; one could study for different exams or attend lectures on a variety of subjects. Anyone who could contribute, did. It was the only way to keep one's mind from becoming hopelessly sluggish.[5]

Although in February 1942 there were attempts to negotiate a prisoner exchange between the Germans and the British, this came to nothing, and Elsie Tilney remained at Vittel for the duration of the war. With her Nonconformist Christian missionary background, it seems unlikely that she availed

---

4   Sofka Skipwith, *The Autobiography of a Princess*, Rupert Hart-Davis, London, 1968, p. 200.

5   Skipwith, *Autobiography*, p. 201.

herself of many of the cultural and educational opportunities celebrated by Sofka Skipwith. In 1943 Elsie's church in Norwich heard that she was suffering from malnutrition.

On 23 January 1943, 198 Polish Jews arrived from Warsaw, followed by 61 more on 22 May. These were survivors of the Warsaw ghetto, and of the rising there in April triggered by the Nazis' attempt to deport the ghetto's remaining Jews to Auschwitz. This latest group of inmates was housed separately from the West European internees in the unfortunately named Hôtel de la Providence. During the same period Jewish prisoners – all apparently of Polish origin – also arrived at Vittel from Drancy transit camp; from Gleiwitz (Gliwice), a sub-camp of Auschwitz; from Westerbork transit camp in the Netherlands; and from Mechelen (Mecheln) deportation camp in Belgium. Russian and Libyan Jewish women and children also arrived. The Libyans had been taken prisoner by Rommel's Afrika Korps and were subsequently transferred to extermination camps, where all lost their lives.

At its height it is reckoned that between 400 and 450 Jewish prisoners were held at Vittel. Many had been issued with papers for emigration to Latin American countries, or were expecting documents from Zionist organizations to enable them to emigrate to Palestine. In the event, the South American governments declined to recognize the authenticity of their documents and refused to admit them.

One young Jewish prisoner from Poland described to an internee named Madeleine White how peasants had pulled him from a mass grave into which he had been thrown with his parents. He was the sole survivor. This story stunned a small group of Englishwomen at Vittel into a new awareness of the dangers that threatened the Jewish prisoners. From this point, these few courageous women showed concern for the Jewish prisoners and attempted to organize internal resistance, for which they were threatened with reprisals.

The commandant at Vittel was Otto Landhäuser, an artillery officer from Innsbruck, Austria, who had previously worked as a physical education instructor. Although he ran a relatively lenient regime for the Western internees, there was no such tolerance for the new Jewish prisoners, whose health problems he instructed the camp's doctors to ignore.

Most of the Jewish prisoners spoke only Yiddish or Polish, so Sofka Skipwith and some of her friends, including Madeleine White, Laura Hannagan and the American Mary Berg, organized English lessons, which they hoped might help them to integrate within the camp or in an English-speaking country, should they later be able to emigrate. At Christmas, some of the interned children put on a show for the Polish Jews during which they performed a Warsaw revolutionary song, for which the British organizers were punished.

By now Miss Tilney was working in the administrative office of the camp, the *Kommandantur*. Many of the Jewish internees had foreign passports (often obtained through the black market), which afforded them some temporary protection. Elsie may have been able to conceal the true origin of some of these Jewish internees. She apparently also discovered that the architects of the Final Solution, Alois Brunner and Adolf Eichmann, had ordered Commandant Landhäuser to separate the Warsaw Jews from the other internees and arrange for them to be transported. In January 1944 Landhäuser moved them to the Hôtel Beau Site, well away from the main camp and

227

accessed by a walkway across a road. In March 1944 a train with boarded-up windows arrived at Vittel, ready to transport these Polish prisoners.

At dawn on 18 April 1944 the Hôtel Beau Site was surrounded by German troops, triggering distress and panic among its Jewish inmates. A number of them attempted suicide by jumping from high windows or stairwells; some were killed outright while others sustained injuries such as broken limbs and ribs. A doctor named Bauminger distributed poison to a number of fellow prisoners; he and his wife died, while his daughter Felicia and another family became seriously ill. German guards loaded 169 Jews on the first train, Transport No. 72, which departed the same day for Drancy. Ten days later, on 29 April, these prisoners were transported from Drancy to Auschwitz, where they were gassed on arrival. Those on this train included the Polish poet Itzhak Katzenelson (1886–1944) and his son Zvi. While at Vittel, Katzenelson wrote in Yiddish *Dos lid funem oysgehargetn yidishn folk* ('Song of the Murdered Jewish People'), a long poem which includes the following stanzas:

I had a dream,
A dream so terrible;
My people were no more,
No more!

I wake up with a cry:
What I had dreamed was true:
It had happened indeed,
It had happened to me.

He hid the manuscript in bottles, which he buried under a tree at Vittel. It was recovered after the war and the poem has subsequently been translated into a number of languages.

After the convoy left, Landhäuser accused some of the Englishwomen of having aided the Polish Jews, and confined Sofka Skipwith and several others to their rooms for a month.

A second boarded-up train, accompanied by SS operatives, arrived a month later, adding further to the despair and panic. On the morning of 16 May at least 52 Polish detainees, including patients on stretchers, suicide survivors and children, were loaded into the sealed trucks and dispatched to Drancy. On 30 May this train, Transport 75, left Drancy for Auschwitz. All were gassed on arrival.

'Miss Tilney was working in the *Kommandantur* on the internees' documents and files; I was frightened of her, suspicious,' Shulamit Troman, a teenage Jewish survivor of Vittel remembered. She naturally suspected her of being a collaborator, complicit with the Nazis. The teenager remembered Tilney as 'very thin', 'withdrawn' and 'very religious – *rétrécie* (tense)', and described an extraordinary encounter:

> I was walking along a corridor when I noticed Miss Tilney coming towards me. I was nervous, because I knew she worked in the *Kommandantur*, and wanted to keep my distance. As she got closer to me, I became more anxious. Then a very strange thing happened. Just as she reached me, she fell to her knees, reached out, took my hand and kissed it. This left me feeling *estomaquée* – flabbergasted – I didn't know what to do or say. Then Miss Tilney said,

'I know you are part of the people who will save the world; you are one of the chosen people.'[6]

Here I was, hoping that no one would know my secret, that I was Jewish, and not really British. Can you imagine how terrifying that was, what it could mean?

Shulamit had been concerned that the Germans would re-classify her as 'stateless' rather than British, making it likely she would be deported. Elsie Tilney told her, 'Don't worry, I will look after you, I will do everything to protect you.' Shulamit added, 'It was very strange. For everyone else, being a Jew was danger, but for Miss Tilney it was special.' After this encounter, Tilney apparently kept a protective eye on the young girl.

The North Africa Mission newsletter recorded that Elsie 'hid for a period of 16 weeks a young Jew condemned to be sent to an annihilation camp in Poland'. This was Sasha Krawech, a Polish machine-gunner who had taken the pseudonym Sasha Heymann and survived the Warsaw ghetto by claiming to be South African. Elsie had been teaching him English and, to help him escape the transports to the east, apparently hid him for five months in her bathroom. He suddenly reappeared on 18 September 1944, when the American army liberated the camp.

Sofka Skipwith had realized Krawech was missing and guessed that Tilney might be involved. Afterwards she wrote:

We felt that Miss Tilney, a middle-aged worker in the *Kommandantur* who had been extremely friendly with

---

6   Such views are similar to those of the ten Boom family and of Jehovah's Witnesses, as described in the Introduction and Chapter 4 above.

Sasha, must have some part in this . . . I went to see her in her room – one of the better ones on the first floor with a bathroom of her own. I told her that if she were in touch with Sasha and he wanted to join the Resistance, we could arrange for him to be collected. It was only after the camp was liberated that it was discovered that he had spent those months in her bathroom . . .

His real name was Krawech. He had joined the Heymann family to replace an already deported son. In 1939 he had been a machine-gunner in the Polish army. After that he was taken prisoner, had gone through the army camps, forced labour camps and each time had managed to come out alive. He had been taken to the terrible Pawiak prison[7] in Warsaw and forced with fifteen others to run up and down between rifle butts swung at them by the German soldiers. After this he had been stripped and one side of him had been painted black. Of the fifteen only five had remained alive – Sasha was one. Fourteen times he had faced certain death of this kind before coming to Vittel. This last escape was the fifteenth.

Another account claims that the young Pole found Miss Tilney 'an old, devoutly Protestant, English spinster . . . so annoying that he was almost driven to give himself up'. An internee also told Elsie Tilney's brother Albert that someone at Vittel informed on her, accusing her of concealing a female Jew – but she was able to deny this with a clear conscience as this was not an accurate description of Krawech.

---

7 Operated by the Gestapo.

Shulamit Troman recalled that:

[Elsie Tilney was] one of the bravest persons I have ever met. She took direct action to save [Krawech]. All of a sudden, six months later, there he was in the yard, white-skinned, exhausted, half-crazy, at his wits' end. He was like a drugged crazy person, but he was alive, saved by Miss Tilney. And then we learned how she saved him, told him if there was another transport he should give her a sign, which he did, and she summoned him to her, which he did, dressed as a woman . . . That is what Miss Tilney did . . . *Une femme remarquable.*

'When the Germans abandoned the camp in September [1944],' another witness recorded, '[Miss Tilney] again put herself in great personal danger by hiding the camp records and papers, for she had been camp archivist.' This was presumably an effort to preserve the records so that justice could be served and history accurately written.

A handful of Jewish prisoners lived through the experience of Vittel internment camp. An internee named Hillel Seidman survived first by hiding in a bread oven and then by concealing himself for several months in empty rooms. 'At the liberation of the camp, I rushed to the Vittel synagogue, which had reopened,' he recalled. 'I could not pronounce the blessing, because it has to be recited by at least ten men.[8] Only then did I realize I was alone, terribly alone.'

---

8   In Jewish tradition a *minyam* (public prayer) requires a quorum of ten men.

Elsie remained at Vittel after the Germans had abandoned the camp in September 1944, and stayed to help some 200 Jewish internees emigrate to Palestine. Before returning to the Baptist church in Paris to restore possessions to some fellow internees, she worked for a month as secretary in an American Rest Hostel. After the war Elsie Tilney worked with the Swiss Mission in Basutoland, South Africa. In retirement she moved to Coconut Grove, Miami-Dade County, Florida, USA, where she settled near her homeopath brother Frederick, who had emigrated to America in the 1920s. Elsie Tilney died in the USA in 1974.

According to the archivist of Surrey Chapel, Dr Rosamunde Codling:

> We are still not one hundred per cent certain of the role Elsie played in the camp, but she had obviously gained enough confidence from the German officials to be involved in administration. The thing that amazes me is that in doing so she would obviously have put herself in a very difficult position with all the other inmates. She would have been seen to be collaborating with the Germans. It is a very fine line, yet she was doing it out of her own convictions and her confidence that she would be able to help Jewish people by maintaining that administrative role. The only thing we can assume is that she was specifically trying to hide their background . . . Elsie used her position to protect them.

Elsie Tilney was honoured as one of the Righteous Among the Nations at Yad Vashem in Israel on 29 September 2013.

Sofka Skipwith was also honoured for saving several Jews and for sending back to Britain a list, in tiny handwriting on thin cigarette paper, of Jews for whom she requested visas.

Bibliography

David Cesarani, *Final Solution: The fate of the Jews 1933–49*, Pan, London, 2017.

Laurence Rees, *The Holocaust*, Penguin, London, 2017.

Nikolaus Wachsmann, *KL: A history of the Nazi concentration camps*, Little, Brown, London, 2015.

The Righteous

Martin Gilbert, *The Righteous: The unsung heroes of the Holocaust*, Black Swan, London, 2011.

Carol Rittner, Stephen D. Smith and Irena Steinfeldt, eds, *The Holocaust and the Christian World: Reflections of the past, challenges for the future*, Continuum, New York, New York, 2000.

Groups

Peter Grose, *A Good Place to Hide: How one French village saved thousands of lives during World War II*, Nicholas Brealey, London, 2016.

Caroline Moorehead, *Village of Secrets: Defying the Nazis in Vichy France*, Chatto & Windus, London, 2014.

Mother Maria

Sergei Hackel, *Pearl of Great Price: The life of Mother Maria Skobtsova*, Darton, Longman & Todd, rev. edn, London, 1982.

Michael Plekon, *Living Icons: Persons of faith in the Eastern Church*, University of Notre Dame Press, Notre Dame, IN, 2002.

Hugh Grimes and Frederick Collard

Helen Fry, *Spymaster: The secret life of Kendrick*, CreateSpace, Scotts Valley, CA, 2014.

Giles MacDonogh, *1938: Hitler's gamble*, Constable, London, 2009.

Jane Haining

David McDougall, ed. Ian Alexander, *Jane Haining*, The Church of Scotland World Mission, Edinburgh, 1998.

Mary Miller, *Jane Haining: A life of love and courage*, Birlinn, Edinburgh, 2019.

Corrie ten Boom

Corrie ten Boom with John and Elizabeth Sherrill, *The Hiding Place*, Hodder & Stoughton, London, 1971.

Hans Poley, *Return to the Hiding Place*, Nova Publishing, Newton Abbot, 1993.

Elisabeth Abegg

Silent Heroes, German Resistance Memorial Center Foundation, Berlin, 2018.

Bruno Reynders

Johannes Blum, *Résistance: Père Bruno Reynders, juste des nations*, Les Carrefours de la Cité, Brussels, 1993.

Hugh O'Flaherty

Owen Chadwick, *Britain and the Vatican during the Second World War*, Cambridge University Press, Cambridge, 1986.

Stephen Walker, *Hide & Seek*, HarperCollins, London, 2011.

Elsie Tilney

Philippe Sands, *East West Street*, Weidenfeld & Nicolson, London, 2017.

Index

Note: Page numbers in **bold** indicate images.

Abegg, Elisabeth 124–47, **143**
Abegg, Julie 142
Amersfoort concentration camp 113
Anschluss 53, 54, 56, 81
Ardeatine Caves massacre 197, **198**
Arrow Cross 82, 86, 90
Aryanization 55, 66
Assisi 2
Auschwitz 30, 36, 63, 94–100, **96**, 128, 150–63, **156**, 189, 202, 226, 228

baptism controversy 176, 178
baptismal certificates 32, 33, 56–9, 204
Batty, Revd Basil, Bishop of Fulham 60, 66, 70
Beje, the 105, **106**, 111–15
Bell, George, Bishop of Chichester 53, 67, 71
Berg, Albert Van den 167, 168, 170–2
Bergen-Belsen 121
Berlin 62, 124–47, 201–17
Besançon 222
Bettelheim, Margaret 69
Birkenau *see* Auschwitz
Birraux, Magda 84
Blake, William 2
Bletchley Park 189
Bloom, Anthony of Sourozh 22, 48
Blumenthal, Hertha 147
Blutschutzgesetz 51, 54

Bogdanska, Kazimera 162
Bovensiepen, Otto 68
Brussels 164, 168, 173–5
Buchenwald 42
Buchholz, Ruth 220, 222
Budapest 70, 75–94, 101–3

Calvinism 7, 109
Chabannes, Château de xii, **xiii**, xiv
Chaillet, Pierre 30
Chevetogne Abbey 178
Christ Church, Vienna 50, 52, 58, 60, 65
Collard, Revd Frederick **57**, 59–61, 63–6, 72–3
Collm, Ludwig 138–40
Collm, Steffi 133, 138–40
Comité de Défense des Juifs 166
Compiègne xv, 30, 39, 40
Confessing Church, Germany 202, 204
Cook, Jean xiv

Dachau 55, 56
Dannecker, Captain Theodor 188
Danube, river 54, 83, 103
David, Star of 33, 89, 93, 111, 127, 128
DELASEM 195, 198
Denmark 6
Derry, Major Sam 181, 186, 194
Deutsche Christen 37

Index

Dobbeck, Margrit 134, 135
Don, Alan 71
Dora camp 41
Drancy 36, 224, 226, 228
Dunscore 103
Dutch Reformed Church 108
Eichmann, Adolf 33, 63, **64**, 89
Eidem, Archbishop Erling 204, 206
Evelyn, Revd F. A. 66, 67, 70

Factory Action 132
Fluchtsteuer 56, 63
Fö utca prison 92, 94
Foley, Frank 62
Forell, Revd Birger 202, 205
Frankl, André 220
Freud, Sigmund 49, 55
Furman, Lieut. John 194
Fürstenberg 40

Gainer, Donald St Clair 58
Georgievsky, Bishop Evlogy 24, 25
German Christians *see Deutsche Christen*
Gestapo 39, 60, 64, 65, 116, 126, 132, 133, 150, 171, 187, 196, 213, 216
Ghiron, Ines 195
Girard-Clot, André xiv, xv
Goebbels, Josef 202, 224
Goldstein, Herta 137
Goldstein, Jack 174
Goldstein, Rachelle 173
Grenoble xii, xiv
Grimes, Revd Hugh 49–59, **57**, 61, 68–73
Grüber, Pastor Heinrich 204
Grüber Office 204
Guernsey 72, 73
Gypsies *see* Romani, Sinti

Haarlem 105, 106, 109, 114
Haining, Jane 74–103, **78**, **91**
Hammerschmidt, Wolfgang 216
Harnack, Ernst von 144
Hartmann, Margarete 135
Hedenqvist, Pastor Göte 203
Henderson, Sir Nevile 61
Herzfeld, Charlotte 144
Heydrich, Reinhard 53
Hiding Place, The 104, 108
Himmler, Heinrich 5, 53, 153
Hirschberg, Anna 130, 131
Hodbomont 167
Hoffmann, Hans 38
homosexuals 3
Hongerwinter 121
Hungarian Reformed Church 87, 101

Jebb, Gladwyn 69
Jehovah's Witnesses 3–5
Jerusalem 6
Jewish Mission Committee, Church of Scotland 75, 86, 87
Jewish Mission Committee School 75, 101, 103
Jugendlager 45, 47

Kaltenbrunner, Ernst 188
Kammerling, Walter 54
Kappler, Herbert 187, 188, 196, 200
Katzenelson, Itzhak 228
Kendrick, Thomas 56, 58, 60–3, 69, 71
Kerkhofs, Monsignor Louis-Joseph 166, 171
Kistarcsa 94
Kleiner, Arthur 68
Klepinin, Father Dimitri 32, 35, 37–41, 48

240

Index

Klepper, Jochen 209
Knies, Hildegard 126, 127, 133,
  137–9, 147
Knight, Revd George A. 70, 81–3, 88
Kornfeld, Paul xi
Krawech, Sasha 230–2
Krygiev, Esther 174

Landhauser, Otto 227, 229
Lang, Archbishop Cosmo 70
Lascroux, Rosane 43
Le Chambon-sur-Lignon 2
Lebensborn programme 157, 161
Lee, Frances 85, 92, 93
Lengyel, Olga 95, 98
Leopoldstadt 54
Lepkifker, Rabbi Joseph 166
Leszczyńska, Bronisław 148, 150
Leszczyńska, Stanisława 148–63,
  149, 158
Leszczyńska, Sylwia 150
Levi, Gertrude 95
Linde, Richard 127, 135, 138
Lisrobin 181
Litzmannstadt *see* Łódź
Livingstone, Laura 204
Lochenhead 74
Łódź 148–50, **151**, 162, 163, 222
Lourmel, rue de 25, 26, **27**, 28, 31,
  34, 37–9
Louvain 164, 167, 168
Luisen-Oberlyzeum 125–7, 131
Lyon xv

Mackenzie, Revd Dr George 75, 80
Maglione, Cardinal Luigi 184
Maltzan, Maria Gräfin von 210–13
Marie-Benoît, Father 195, 196
Mattick, Friedrich 215, 217

Mauthausen xv, 150
Meisel, Lucian 53
Mengele, Josef 4, 153, 155
MI6 51, 56, 69
Mildmay Mission to the Jews 219
Mont César 164, 165, 167
Montpellier xv
Mossel, Meijer 113
Muckermann, Father Friedrich 211
Mundfunk 130
Mussolini 182
Myrgren, Revd Erik 201, 202,
  213–18

Nagy, Revd Dr Louis Nagybaczoni
  87, 88, 101
Neuengamme concentration camp
  172
Neumann, Oskar 69
Neumann, Ralph 141, **143**
Neumann, Rita 141, 142
Newton Ferrers 72
Niewiadomska, Leokadia 161
Noisy-le-Grand 27, 34
North Africa Mission 220, 230
Norwich 219
Nosovich, Sophia 44

O'Flaherty, Monsignor Hugh
  180–200, **184, 199**
Ohmann, Vide 205, 206, **207**, 208
Oranienburg 3
Osborne, Sir Francis d'Arcy
  Godolphin 181, 182, 186, 190,
  192, 193, 200
Oświęcim *see* Auschwitz

Packard, Katalin 80, 89
Palestine 57, 63, 136, 72, 198, 226

Index

Panton, Revd David 220
Paragraph 175 3
Paris xi, 24–40, 45
Pawlowska, Elzbieta 160
Pereles, Liselotte 132, 142, 145
Perichon, Solange 44
Perl, Gisella 153
Perwe, Revd Erik 202, 204–13, **207**
Pery, Jacqueline 47
Pilenko, Elizaveta *see* Skobtsova,
    Maria
Pilenko, Sophia 23
pink triangle 3
Pitt-River, George Lane-Fox 65, 67
Pius XII, Pope 184, **185**
Poelchau, Pastor Harald 142
Poley, Johannes 113
Pollitzer, Edmund 61, 63
Popper, Dr Stefan 69
Prague xi
Prém, Margit 83, 87, 98, 99, 101
Pritchard, Marion 8
Pulasy, Erwin 72

Quakers 125–7, 144, 205

Ravasz, Bishop László 90, 93, 101
Ravensbrück 42, 45, **46**, 119–21, **120**
Red Cross, International 47, 99, 162,
    216
Resistance xii, xiv, 30, 34, 116
Reyevsky, George 31, 32
Reynders, Dom Bruno 164–79, **169**,
    177
Richter, Fred 62, 63
Righteous Among the Nations xv, 9,
    10, 22, 48, 62, 103, 123, 147, 166,
    172, 178, 217, 233
Robinsohn, Hans 125

Roda, Edit 82
Roeg, Cardinal van 166
Romani 3, 5
Rome 180–200
Roncalli, Angelo 186
Rotmil, Bernard 170
Rozberg, Gilles 172
Rückert-Gymnasium 126

SA *see Sturmabteilung*
Sachsenhausen 3
Sacred Congregation of the Holy
    Office 181
St Michel du Valle 72
St-Romain-et-St-Clément xii
Saloman, Maria 159
Sands, Philippe 222
Saussaies, rue de 38
Scheveningen 117, 118
Schmitz, Elisabeth 134
Schönhaus, Samson 136
Schréder 90
Schutzstaffel 5, 187, 229
Schwedenmöbel 213
Schwersenz, Jizchak 136, 147
Scotland, Church of 100, 101
SD *see Sicherheitsdienst*
Secret Intelligence Service *see* MI6
Seidman, Hillel 232
Sicherheitsdienst 38
Siemens-Halske 42
Simpson, Lieut. Bill 194
Singer-Mendalavitz, Flora 172, 175
Sinti 3
Siöcrona, Meri 206, 217
SIS *see* MI6
Skipwith, Sofka 224–7, 229–31
Skobtsov, Yuri 40–2, 48
Skobtsova, Danilo 23

Index

Skobtsova, Maria 22–48, **29**
Snedden, Father Owen 183, 194
Sonderkommando 97
SS *see Schutzstaffel*
Stettin 201, 213
Strassmann, Ernst 125
Sturmabteilung 54
Surányi, Ibolya 79, 102
Surrey Street Chapel, Norwich 219, 222
Svábhegy prison 92
Swedish Victoria Church, Berlin 202, **203**, 206–10, 213–17
Szabo, Judith 77

Tec, Nechama 7
Tempelhof Airport 209, 215
ten Boom, Betsie 105, 112, 117, 118, 121
ten Boom, Casper 105, 111, 112, 114, 117
ten Boom, Corrie (Cornelia) 104–23, **107**
ten Boom, Nollie 105, 116, 117
ten Boom, Willem 105, 108, 117
Terezín 128, **129**
Theresienstadt *see* Terezín
Tilney, Elsie 219–34, **221**
Treblinka 69
Troman, Shulamit 229, 230
Tucek, Karl 63

U-boats 128, 129, 136, 205, 213

Vatican 182, 190–3, 196
Vatican Lines 180
Vélodrome d'Hiver 35
Vichy 183
Vienna 49–71, 203, 220
Vincent, Pastor Henri 220
Vittel 222–33, **223**
Vörösmarty utca 51, **76**
Vught, Kamp 118, 119

Wannsee Conference 5, 184
Weidenfeld, George 72
Weissenberg, Martin and Margot 215
Weizsäcker, Ernst von 190, 196
Wendland, Agnes 141
Wendland, Ruth 134, 141, **143**
Wesslén, Eric 206, 213–15
Westerweel, Joop 8, 9
Westphal, Charles xiv
White, Madeleine 226, 227
Wlach, Oskar 69

Yad Vashem xv, 6, 9, 10, 22, 48, 103, 123, 166, 178, 233

Zeisl, Egon 68
Zeisl, Erich 68
Zyklon B 128